CRITICAL ACCLAIM
The Secret L

'A well written and powerful voice in the grand movement
to rescue us from the empty secularism of our society
by discovering the soul'
M. Scott Peck, bestselling author of *The Road Less Travelled*

'Keith Miller is one of the original thinkers on spiritual personality
theory . . . In *The Secret Life of the Soul* [he] points the way
towards awareness, integrity, and a healing faith'
T. George Harris, *Editor, Spirituality and Health* Magazine

'Keith Miller's journey through brokenness is a journey that
most of us must take . . . He has blazed a trail that many
of us can follow . . .'
Tony Campolo, Professor of Sociology, Eastern College,
St Davids, Pennsylvania

'*The Secret Life of the Soul* is an honest, revealing, and very
courageous book – full of insight for authentic spiritual
growth and realistic hope'
Howard E. Butt, Jr, author of *Renewing America's Soul*

'What a treasure this book is for all who search for a sense
of self-worth, authenticity and God'
George Gallup, Jr, Chairman, George H. Gallup International Institute,
Executive Director, Princeton Research Center, and author of
The Saints Among Us

'Keith Miller's brilliant book brings his fresh and personal
approach to the search for the soul. It will be an enormous
help to many'
Bruce Larson, author of *What is God Asking You?*

ALSO BY J. KEITH MILLER

The Taste of New Wine

A Second Touch

Habitation of Dragons

The Becomers

The Edge of Adventure (with Bruce Larson)

Living the Adventure (with Bruce Larson)

The Passionate People (with Bruce Larson)

Please Love Me

The Single Experience (with Andrea Wells Miller)

The Scent of Love

The Dream

Hope in the Fast Lane (previously published as
Sin: Overcoming the Ultimate Deadly Addiction)

Facing Co-dependence
(with Pia Mellody and Andrea Wells Miller)

*A Hunger for Healing: The 12 Steps as a Classical Model for
Christian Spiritual Growth*

Facing Love Addiction
(with Pia Mellody and Andrea Wells Miller)

Highway Home Through Texas

Ten Minute Magic: Uncovering and Achieving Your Dreams

THE SECRET LIFE
OF THE SOUL

J. Keith Miller

BANTAM BOOKS

LONDON · NEW YORK · TORONTO · SYDNEY · AUCKLAND

THE SECRET LIFE OF THE SOUL
A BANTAM BOOK : 0553 81236 X

First publication in Great Britain

PRINTING HISTORY
Bantam edition published 1999

Set in 10 on 13pt Sabon by
Phoenix Typesetting, Ilkley, West Yorkshire.

Bantam Books are published by Transworld Publishers Ltd,
61–63 Uxbridge Road, London W5 5SA,
in Australia by Transworld Publishers (Australia) Pty Ltd,
15–25 Helles Avenue, Moorebank, NSW 2170,
and in New Zealand by Transworld Publishers (NZ) Ltd,
3 William Pickering Drive, Albany, Auckland.

Reproduced, printed and bound in Great Britain by
Cox & Wyman Ltd, Reading, Berks.

Contents

*'The meaning of earthly existence is not, as
we have grown used to thinking, in prosperity,
but in the development of the soul.'*
Alexander Solzhenitsyn

To contact J. Keith Miller about speaking engagements, write
or call Michael McKinney, McKinney Associates, Inc.,
P.O. Box 5162, Louisville, KY 40205, (800) 955-4746.

Acknowledgments

WITH REGARD TO THE PERSONAL ILLUSTRATIONS IN THIS book, I have shamelessly fictionalized them with reference to identities, locations, sexes, and exact dialogue in order to protect peoples' anonymity. But in every case the emotional event happened to someone, even where the physical circumstances are unrecognizable. I am very grateful to the many people who have shared experiences and given me permission to use them in this way.

I am also grateful to the summer adult class at St Matthews church in Austin, Texas, where the basic material in this book was first delivered as a series of talks.

Since this book is so personal and yet also deals with some concepts and classical ideas that have been floating around forever, I felt a real need for help from friends whose knowledge and insight I respect, most of whom also know me well enough to see past my denial.

The following people read all or parts of this book in manuscript form and gave me invaluable positive criticisms and ideas. I didn't take all their suggestions, so I can't blame them for any errors that may still be in the book. Since these are all very busy people, who took the time to do this reading, I am filled with gratitude as I write these words. I honestly don't know if I would ever have finished this book without the help and encouragement of these friends: Victor Appel, Carter Birely, Christina Felker, Paul Franklin, John and Barry French, George Gallup, Jr, Ed and Noel Gerlich, Brooks Goldsmith, Richard Gersuch, John K. Graham, Richard D. Grant Jr, T. George Harris, Lilas and John Harvey, Francis (Doc) Heatherly, Earl Henslin, Fred Hill, Howard and Carol Houde, Carolyn and Chuck Hoffman, Earl Koile, Madeleine L'Engle, Bruce Larson, Don Matthews, Martha T. Miller, Robert (Chip) Nix, M. Scott Peck, Eugene Peterson, Paul Rush and Vicki Spencer.

I also want to thank people who took time to read the manuscript and make any comments that may appear on the jacket or front pages of the book.

Special thanks go to Karen Wood, who offered to help even though she was very sick. Karen died before the book went to press.

Also, I can't say enough about my friend and agent, Kathleen Niendorff, who not only is a wonderful literary representative, but who kept giving me positive suggestions, and assurances that there was a book in the midst of it all.

I'm grateful to our friend Sharon Tomisak for the wonderful gift of typing the audio tapes of the lectures and researching sources on the Internet, and to Jan Elliott Cronk and Kim White for helping us to stay afloat in the rest of our life while the book-storm swirled around us all.

Finally, I want to thank my daughter, Mary-Keith Dickinson, and my wife, Andrea Wells Miller, for encouraging me from the beginning, saying that what the book has to say would be worth the risk of writing it as I did.

Andrea is in many ways coauthor. She helped me structure and clarify the original lectures at every point in the process. When the shaming voices and my own sinful need to be invulnerable and to stay in control made me start to reach and preach at the reader instead of witnessing to what I have seen and heard, she saw through my grandiosity and helped me get back on track.

It is to these two wonderful women, Andrea and Mary-Keith, that this book is dedicated.

J. Keith Miller
Austin, Texas.

THE SECRET LIFE
OF THE SOUL

Introduction

A NUMBER OF PEOPLE HAVE TOLD ME RECENTLY THAT somehow the spiritual adventure, and life in general, have gone dead for them, that their faith has not been able to solve their inner difficulties. They turn their problems over to God, but God seems to leave them untouched. They don't know whether this is due to the inadequacy of their faith or to their own inability to deal with their lives and relationships. Many people, through spiritual groups in churches, through the twelve-step programs, and in counselling sessions, have realized there's a previously undiscovered level of life going on inside themselves. Evidently a lot of us are in serious denial about our personal and spiritual issues.

This is a book about the soul and the search for self-esteem, authenticity, and God. It deals with basic spiritual problems that have found a common landing place in the church and in the lives of sensitive men and women everywhere.

In these pages I want to take you with me into very private

inner areas of experience, where great wars rage that we often don't talk about. Here the battles to love and be loved are rehearsed and recapitulated. In this inner arena we do our serious worrying, trying to figure things out. Eventually we come to realize, to our surprise, that our spiritual problems don't respond well to cognitive analysis. This is where we encounter our soul, the childlike yet wise part of us that is the spiritual experiencing center, and where we hear also some *inner* voices, strident and shaming, that say, 'You're no good! You're inadequate! You're dumb! You're unattractive!' 'Too fat.' 'Too thin!' Here in the privacy of our interior lives these two parts of us – the soul and the shaming voices – wage their terrible debates about our value as a person. Unfortunately we often pay more attention to the shaming voices that tell us that we're really not 'enough.' We don't feel good about ourselves and may even lose hope.

Actually these pages have been written for anyone who is on a serious spiritual search. But the book will be most relevant to you if your own spiritual searching has bogged down:

- because you find that although you are a serious religious person, even converted, you are still plagued with fears, insecurities, and low self-esteem;
- because you made a serious commitment of your life to God at some time, but life and your faith have become boring or prosaic and not happy or energized;
- because of some depressing or painful personal failure, or the failure of the promises you felt were implicit in the faith you once held, or are trying to hold; or
- because you can't seem to 'get in touch' with God, people close to you, or any strong sense of security about what you want to do with the rest of your life.

I want to say three things right off. First, this is not intended to be the definitive work on the soul. What you will find in these pages has been helpful to me in making sense out of the human spirit. Second, you should know that I do not believe the type of spiritual journey I will describe in these pages is for everyone, or is a requirement for being a spiritual person or a Christian.

And third, after much study and research it is apparent to me that no one knows what the soul actually 'looks like' or indeed that it 'exists' in a physical sense (although a group of scientists have reported that they have 'found discrete locations in the brain of an intricate system that serves, among other things, as the human moral compass. Largely in the prefrontal cortex, it is . . . where our personal scales of justice do their weighing.'[1]) But for all practical purposes the soul is still a mystery To investigate the soul in any concrete sense, we must reach into the black box and talk about something we cannot see or touch or posit, as scientists must about certain activity inside an atom.

A friend who heard that I was going to try to describe the life of the soul reminded me of an old story about a little boy who was intensely drawing a picture. His mother asked, 'What are you drawing a picture of?'

'God,' the little boy said.

With a concerned look, the mother said, carefully, 'Honey, no one knows what God looks like.'

Without missing a beat or even looking up, the boy announced with great confidence, 'Well, they will when I finish this picture!'

Because of the turmoil and insecurity resulting from the inner warfare I will describe, it would be difficult to present a clear picture of the soul and its activities, even if a clear picture existed. Following the Hebrew practice of making spiritual realities concrete through drama, I will try to present the soul in the context of its adventure in the spiritual journeys of stressed men and women in a largely materialistic culture.

In order to penetrate some of the fog caused by the denial and inner confusion that often attend the search for the soul I have depicted in simple parables that which cannot be described clearly at all. Years ago Karl Menninger helped me enormously with the dilemma of having to be simplistic in dealing with elusive spiritual issues when he pointed out:

> It may be objected that this sharpness or clarity involves certain distortion or misrepresentation, dependent upon oversimplification. But this is the perennial dilemma of the teacher: the teaching of facts and figures versus the teaching of truth . . . The student must 'learn' things in order to realize subsequently that they are not quite the way he (or she) learned them. By that time the student will have gotten into the spirit of the matter, and from this he (or she) may arrive at some approximation of the truth, an approximation the student will continue to revise all his (or her) life long.[2]

My hope is that you may begin to identify and see something of yourself in my own story and the drama of conflicting inner voices (and forces) I am presenting. But since I believe that each person's drama is in some ways unique, your experience may be quite different from the parts of my life I have used to illustrate the life of the soul. Getting involved in this process several years ago, I found that a deeper truth than I was seeking had grasped me in a personal, intimate way.

In translating this journey from the medium of a personal verbal dialogue to the written page I was confronted with the problem of how to present the adventure of the soul in a way that would help to clarify the inner dynamics without offending the intelligent reader and causing him or her to dismiss the content as being childish. In the following pages I have tried to present, as simply as possible, the way I believe the soul – that most central and mysterious spiritual consciousness – operates as a guide to all kinds of everyday human reality, to self-esteem, and to God. To show a composite picture of the inner dynamics of human spiritual development and experience, I have used a few commonly known ideas of psychology and religion – familiar to even casual students of the literature of those disciplines – as intellectual stage props to present the *inner drama* in which human beings encounter the fear, shame, and failure that drive us this way and that in our deep struggles for self-esteem, love, and reconciliation.

It is not my intention, however, to present a psychological personality theory. Rather, my purposes are spiritual: I have mined my own experiences from a lifetime of seeking, as well as the learnings of many with whom I have counseled and journeyed as we have searched for truth about living out humankind's spiritual quest.

My own life and relationships have changed so significantly during the process I will describe that you may be skeptical and make a 'correction for incredulity.' You may think my problems, my spiritual crises, or the accounts of real continuing recovery so extreme that you can't relate to them. My hope is that you will suspend your skepticism and be open to looking at a different way to experience life and hope and faith.

My own adventure indicates that this search can lead some of us beyond ourselves to the experience of feeling loved by Something – Someone – greater and higher than we could reach even on the tiptoes of our intellects.

J. Keith Miller
Austin, Texas

Part 1

The Source and Pain of Soul Searching

1

The Sight of Blindness

I came into the world to bring everything into the clear light of day, making all distinctions clear, so that those who have never seen will see, and those who have made a great pretense of seeing will be exposed as blind.
John 9:39, *The Message*

THE SUN WAS RISING ON ANOTHER WHITE-HOT TEXAS DAY IN Blanco County. I was in an isolated area of a ranch in the central Texas hill country, sitting on a wooden bench. Before me the sunrise etched in gold the outlines of the Charles Umlauf seventeen-foot bronze statue of Jesus. As I sat in front of that compassionate figure, in the midst of my shattered dreams, I was sobbing.

I stopped crying and hugged myself to keep from shaking. My body ached from the past three years of conflict, pain, and fear. My marriage of twenty-seven years was over . . . finished! My vocational life as a Christian writer and speaker was about to shrivel and atrophy. Yet something else had ended,

9

something even deeper and more frightening: Was it my life? No, I was alive, although I was numb. Still it felt as if the person I'd always imagined myself to be was dying.

I looked down at the beads of red clay soil that made up a large anthill about two feet in front of me. A big rust-colored straggler had happened onto my white sneaker and was making his way onto my bare leg. I started to smash him to keep him from hurting me. Then I remembered my prayer to God, just a moment before, for mercy and guidance, and gently flipped my industrious little companion back to the ground.

I thought back over the last twenty years, trying to sort out how I had come to this place. After making a complete, sincere commitment of my life to God in Jesus Christ twenty years before, I had earnestly sought God's will. I had felt much peace and gratitude as I immersed myself in doing God's work: praying, studying, writing, leading conferences, and helping people. Eventually my first book, *The Taste of New Wine*, sold worldwide. Suddenly I was a minor celebrity. I remembered being very grateful and feeling humble. Life was exciting.

I went to graduate school and completed degrees in theology and in psychology/counseling and wrote another book along the way. During the next few years I wrote nine books about the problems I experienced in trying to live with God as the center of my life. All of them were considered 'Christian best sellers.' I was asked to speak on programs in many parts of the world with some of the outstanding Christians of that time, several of whom became personal mentors. I prayed daily. I read the Scriptures, books about the lives of the saints, and devotional books. I attended worship regularly, tithed, and participated in the work of the church as a layman. I even asked God for the filling of His Spirit and received some peace about having done all I'd heard of to be God's person. The pace was breathless but exhilarating.

One night in September 1969 I was sitting on the stage of a convention center in Minneapolis, looking out on a full house of more than 8,000 people, 4,600 of them delegates to the first U.S. Congress on Evangelism. I was the evening speaker and was being introduced by the honorary chairman, Billy Graham. Although in the photographs I saw later I looked calm, actually my stomach was tight and my mouth was dry. As the introduction continued, my mind flashed back to my childhood in Oklahoma when I'd been sitting watching a sunset by myself, day-dreaming that I would be able to help people someday, perhaps even help them to find God. Now here I was, about to speak to the evangelists of America. I was filled with gratitude and humility. I heard the chairman say my name and beckon me to the podium. The lights were very bright, and I couldn't believe I was the person walking across that stage.

Yet only a few years later I became aware that there was something wrong inside of me. There was a baffling paradox: I was continuing to lead many people to a simpler, more focused life with Christ that was evidently real and life-changing for them, yet my own life lacked clarity, and my complex schedule was suddenly a cold prickly acid fog bank of too many things I'd agreed to do. I was filled with the chaos of not having enough time, and it seemed as if I were wrestling for some kind of survival. Within myself I no longer felt the self-esteem and happiness other 'committed Christians' appeared to feel. Some of them reported finally finding peace and good feelings about themselves as children of God. But, although I was sincerely committed to Christ, I realized that I had taken on a lot more commitments than I could sanely fulfill; I was frantically trying to prepare talks and write books between counseling sessions and speaking engagements. I no longer experienced much peace or many good feelings.

Instead, I realized I was a driven and insecure person inside. Although I was grateful for the success God had given me, I was still afraid of failure and tried hard to do everything right. This surrendered Christian life that I was living was accomplishing many things, but my life inside didn't look like the intimate and centered Jesus of the Bible I read about every day.

During this confusing time I was asked to speak to a convention in Boston. Several prominent Christian writers were on the program. Two nights before the meeting I woke up in the middle of the night. I saw a mental picture of myself speaking at the meeting. Everyone was bored and began visiting with people in the seats next to them. I felt panic. There I was, revealed in front of that large group of learned people as being dull, unintelligent, and inept as a communicator. I lay in my bed, sweating and afraid, imagining my own failure. I thought about God and prayed for peace and guidance. And I remember thinking, 'This is amazing! I have made every commitment I know about of my life to God – but I have almost no trust at all when it comes to my own performance!'

Somehow I had built a larger-than-life personality, in all sincerity, in order to live and work for God. That personality had a kind of ambition and drive that many of my non-Christian associates in business had, and I would have called *their* way of life compulsive to the point of being dysfunctional. Yet I was sincerely committed to living for God. What was going on?

During the next few years following this budding awareness, I continued to travel all over the world speaking and conducting seminars. I realized I had gotten the degree in psychology/counseling at least partially in the hope that I could discover what this inner fear of failure (and success) was all about.

Eventually I went for help to a fine counselor who, after one session, said, 'Keith, you are like an extraordinary pilot who can do amazing things in the air – but you don't seem to know how to land. You need to learn how to stop and rest.' I considered his words and tried to slow down, but when I put down one project, I would take on at least one new one. I had a full speaking schedule and was about to finish writing a book when I agreed to do a sixteen-week radio series in New York. I'd promised myself some rest after the book, but this was an 'important opportunity' for God – and for me.

I was working hard, trying to be a good Christian witness, but I was also striving to do well in my lay ministry in a way that made me uneasy somehow. And in the process I lost touch with those close to me in some semiconscious way. I thought I was just busy giving my best for God, but I began to see that there was an unseen warfare inside of me that had separated my driving, witty, intense self from that simple childlike part I call my soul. Finally I began to suspect that my relationships were not what I thought they were.

One morning at breakfast with my family I was in the midst of trying to justify having taken on yet another speaking commitment – in spite of already having a full schedule and having told my wife I wanted more time at home. Conducting my defense, I said, 'Listen, I *owe* this guy. He came to speak for us at a conference last year. It's an *obligation*!'

As I looked around the table, I saw sad or angry looks. Then as these people closest to me began to get up and go into their day, I suddenly felt very uncomfortable. Although what I had *said* was true, I had a disconcerting moment when I realized two things: First, my real 'priority obligation' was to give some time, attention, and love to the people sitting around that table. And second, I had the unacceptable awareness that the *real* reason I'd accepted the speaking engagement was not that

I had an obligation to, but because it would further my career. Immediately I buried the flicker of awareness that I'd lied to my family; I quickly replayed in my mind the scene of telling my friend a year earlier that I owed him one, thereby satisfying myself that I had been honest. After all, I *had* told my friend the year before, 'Sure, I'll come speak for you some day if you'll do our conference now.' I got up and hurried to get at my work – the awareness that I'd lied was gone.

I still felt humble and grateful for all the opportunities that had come to me, and I was still counseling with hurting people wherever I went. But looking back, I can remember certain changes in me. I found myself mentioning important people I'd been with and filling the silence of our married relationship with my own unconscious grandiosity. So much that I did was centered on me and my work. Although my wife and I took trips together and talked about what was happening, and I spent a lot of time with my family at night, reading to the children and praying with them when I put them to bed, my attention was often focused on my being an 'outstanding Christian.' Inside I sincerely felt like I was being God's person as husband and father. But I can now see that although my strong work ethic served me well, my *behavior* was often that of a success-driven compulsive worker.

Ultimately, in horror, I realized that my relationship with my wife had changed more than I had thought. Communication became very difficult, and even with all my training as a counselor I couldn't fix the relationship. I felt alone, angry, and sad. After a few years the confusion and lonely frustration were killing me. I was afraid I could never get my work done – or my personal life straightened out. I was miserable.

Finally the low point happened when I was disloyal to my wife for the first time ever. Life went from uncomfortable to chaotic and very fearful. After two years of marriage coun-

seling and much anger, fear, and verbal warf?
getting a divorce. Even though I wanted despera
myself, I could not.

So, in April 1976, I was sitting in front of the towering figure
of Jesus in the already radiating morning sunshine, grieving
over the failure of my marriage, my vocation, and the death of
the knight-in-shining-armor I'd tried so hard to be for God.

During the next few years my inner life hit rock bottom
(described later in this book). I thought, prayed, studied, and
counseled others and was counseled, trying always to understand how a person like me – who wanted to be honest with
everyone – could hide the truth from himself, be immoral, be
dishonest with others, and sabotage his own life and career –
all the while still wanting to know and do God's will and be
His witness.

I have counseled about my life with some of the wisest
Christians and psychological counselors I could find. Also
over the past twenty years, Christian leaders, ministers, writers,
and musicians have come to me for help when their marriages and vocations have crashed and burned. As I listened to
these sensitive, intelligent men and women whose lives were
seriously committed to Jesus Christ – and yet who were
now alone and frightened – I began to see some common patterns evolve.

I started to see how men and women who sincerely desire to
be God's people can make all the right verbal and sacramental
commitments and still wind up frightened, lonely, in denial,
and confused about their lives.

I saw that inside our lives, where we seldom take other
people, there is a secret life of the soul, an intimate adventure
that can reveal or hide much of the baffling glory and tragedy
of one's life – even from one's self.

Our Interior Battles

Exactly what are we fighting here? Who are the specific players in our sometimes frightening and shameful inner drama, and how do they talk to each other? In the developing life of the soul that this book describes, one learns to do battle with the inner shaming voices and, with God's help, to receive the gift of experiencing enough self-worth to stand up and win some of the painful daily skirmishes with the limiting and eroding forces in our lives.

Here's a specific example of the way that battle plays out in my life. I had agreed to deliver a series of weekly lectures on which this book is based to an adult class in the church I attend. The morning I was to begin the series I flew home from a trip to meet the class for the first time. As the plane was landing an hour or so before I was to be at the lecture hall, I suddenly felt very insecure about speaking vulnerably to this group, among whom were many well-loved, close friends.

As I drove toward the church, my inner voices taunted me: 'Keith, you're crazy! What in the world are you doing teaching a ten-week series dealing with such emotionally charged material? Besides, you're over the hill. You don't have anything interesting to say to these people about life. Something new for ten weeks? Are you kidding?' Then those voices reminded me, 'Even Jesus never made it in His own home town!'

These sort of messages often come at me when I risk trying something new that my soul urges me to do. If I'm not careful at that moment, I will believe those negative inner voices instead of my soul, and back down – maybe even eliminate from this book some of my own struggles and failures that could help make the reality and possible urgency of your soul's voice clear to you.

Where We're Going

This book is the result of my own pain and study, and the journey toward the greater sense of happiness, peace, and self-esteem I have begun to experience. In these pages I want to take you with me *into* the fray where the mystery of the 'failure of success' takes place. We will examine the process by which good people become separated from their families and their most basic commitments until they come to grips with the unreality of their stress-filled lives.

I hope to blow away the fog and provide a pictorial atlas, a map of this fearful inner territory where our searching takes place. This interior region is the part of our experience where we deny our good character traits as well as our harmful ones, where we make secret and often baffling, self-defeating decisions. This is also where, when we are at our best, we love God and look to Him assiduously for direction to help us grow toward our highest goals.

Sin and Evil

There are two mysterious and powerful invisible forces that every soul encounters in its spiritual search for reality and God.

(1) One is the universal and self-defeating interior bent toward a powerful, rebellious self-centeredness often called 'Sin.' This renegade energy seems to be in opposition to God's benevolent purpose for His creation. Insidiously, and often unconsciously, Sin nudges us to replace God in our personal world, even sometimes as we are consciously trying to find and obey God. From the beginning of life this interior and self-defeating bent can lead a person subtly or openly to control

and abuse people and circumstances in order to be number one, or just to get what he or she wants when a desire is recognized. The late William Temple said that there is only one Sin (with a capital *S*) and it is characteristic of every person. That Sin is putting one's self in the center where only God belongs. All other sins (with a small *s*), like murder, rape, stealing, adultery, and gossip, are things we do because we have put ourselves in the center through this Copernican shift.[1] The baffling part about our experience of Sin is that its primary symptom is 'denial' or the fact that we cannot see its presence in our own lives.

(2) In life there is also a deep and frustrating mystery that we experience as an adversarial force, exerting strong energy – either very subtly or violently – to influence our lives, inside and out, *away from* the search for reality, unselfish love, and God. This invisible force, generally thought of as personal 'evil,' seems to be a part of the fabric of all individual and social life. When people encounter the influence and power of evil personally, it is often experienced in human relationships as someone tried to nudge, lure, or seduce us toward doing something against our highest values or even against our best interest (like controlling, lying, or using people for our own purposes). The experience of this invisible counterforce is so 'personal' that in the Bible it was given a name – Satan – which meant 'the Adversary' (later translated 'the Devil' by the Greeks). The point here is that whether or not one recognizes his or her underlying desire to be number one as 'Sin' or the personally experienced evil as 'Satan,' a practical dilemma is set up for the developing soul.

If one does believe in Sin or Satan, there is a tendency to blame antisocial or self-centered behavior on Satan or Sin and thus deny our personal responsibility to face ourselves and grow. On the other hand, people who do not believe in Sin or personal evil sometimes tend to blame their antisocial behavior on abusive parents, uncaring governments, unfortunate marriages, etc. The point here is that at each step of the way toward spiritual growth of the soul there is a chance to take responsibility and grow – or to deny, blame, and stay stuck in bewildering anxiety and stress. This is not an easy journey. My experience and counseling indicate that sinful acts and evil do not come in clear black-and-white uniqueness, but, rather, marble themselves in the cracks between goodness and the needs for survival, like fat in heavy beefsteaks.

A child's *experience* doesn't come with abstract labels on it – like 'I am Sin,' or 'I am personal evil whose name is Satan.' Therefore I will describe in these pages the way the inner battles for self-esteem may *feel* to *any* child, not just those raised in a theological community. I will try to describe ways in which we may all experience growing up and dealing with our own sinful choices and those of our parents and caregivers, and how the soul – a part of our own imperfect humanity – tries through it all to be guide and encourager, nudging us toward reality and God.

I am aware that a lot of people don't even visit this arena of their inner experience; indeed, they may only have a faint notion of its existence. But even those who long to understand themselves, like I do, are sometimes blind and often do not know how to conceptualize or interpret what goes on in their innermost beings where the soul longs to be heard and loved.

In this book we will examine the spiritual adventure as a secret storyline about the imprisonment of the soul and the inner struggles that can lead us to a glorious liberation and on – or back – to God.

But first, a look at the soul.

2

Photographing the Wind

I AM EXCITED ABOUT TELLING YOU WHAT I HAVE DISCOVERED about the soul. Although people have talked and written about this subject as far back as recorded history goes, attempts at trying to *describe* the soul, this most important character in our spiritual dramas, are almost nonexistent. What we discover as we try to get a picture of the soul from the writings that do exist is a little like seeing photographs of the wind. One can see the *effects* of breezes, windstorms, and blizzards by such discernible signs as the movement of trees, our mussed hair, and flapping clothing, flying debris, and the swirling of rain and snow. But the soul itself, like the wind, can only be seen fleetingly in its actions and its effects on behavior and parts of the human personality.

Webster's dictionary says that the soul is 'the spiritual principle embodied in human beings, all rational and spiritual beings.'[1]

Most of those in our culture who have written about the soul as a real part of life are those who are themselves on a spiritual quest. Besides musicians who have created 'soul' music that expresses the sad and almost unspeakable longings of living and loving, writers about the soul itself have been primarily: (1) biblical writers (and those writing about the Bible) and (2) psychologists.

'Soul' in the Bible

I searched through the Old and New Testaments of the Bible and read the more than 240 references to 'soul' or 'souls.' I was fascinated to see that soul had different but related meanings when used by biblical characters in the course of Hebrew/Christian history. Four different meanings represent about 90 percent of the uses of the word *soul*. Most often the soul is seen simply as the seat of a human being's deepest feelings and human desires (e.g., Gen. 34:3, ['Shechem's] soul was drawn to Dinah,' or Lam. 1:20, 'Behold, O LORD, for I am in distress, my soul is in tumult').

A second use of the word *soul*, occurring about the same number of times, refers to the soul as the seat of a particular spiritual part of our personality that relates to God or the things of God (e.g., Ps. 119:20, 'My soul is consumed with longing for thy ordinances,' or Ps. 146:1, 'Praise the LORD O my soul!').

Seeing the soul as a separate and discrete part of the personality in addition to our mind, strength, and heart is highlighted in several passages (e.g., Luke 10:27, 'You shall love the Lord your God with all your heart, and with all your soul, and with all your strength and with all your mind.' See also Mark 12:30).

A third use of the word *soul* reflects a view that one's highest values are processed by a particular part of the personality (called the soul). This would indicate that what we today call the 'conscience' – that which attempts to remind us of our highest values – would be an integral part of the soul.

The soul can affect our thinking as well as our behavior regarding every area of our lives. Logical facts can be deceiving when one is making important personal decisions about things like who to marry or what vocation to choose. The soul has an intuitive grasp of reality that takes logical arguments into consideration, but urges us to make decisions about proposed changes of behavior and direction for living at a deeper, more intuitional and personally comprehensive level. The soul always seems to relate potential choices to one's *values* and nudges us to go beyond the purely rational toward personal integrity. Jesus kept pointing to the different quality of this deeper perspective about life. But the Pharisees and Saducees had a lot of trouble with this shift from the strictly rational to the spiritual world that Jesus was presenting. Nicodemus, a wise leader of the Jews, came to Jesus at night, wanting to understand the truth for his soul. He was a real left-brainer with a graduate school mentality. He came to Jesus and said, in effect, 'I really believe what You're saying. It sounds good to me, true – and of God. But I don't quite understand it. Could you explain it to me again? You're talking about a whole revolution of life, aren't You?'

Jesus said, 'Nicodemus, you must be born again.'

We can almost see Nicodemus trying to figure that one out. He said, 'You mean I've got to go back up inside my mother's womb?'

But Jesus said, in effect: What I'm talking about is so different from the way you've been educated that you're going to have to die to that way of thinking in order to see the spiritual drama that is the real life I'm talking about. (See John 3:1–10.)

The fourth most frequent use of *soul* in the Bible points to that part of us that is thought to continue after this life. During most of biblical history the writers didn't portray life after death as being the joyful place and state that heaven connotes to most people since the New Testament was written. When people died they went to Sheol, the land of shadows (e.g., Ps. 30:3, 'O Lord thou hast brought up my soul from Sheol.'). But the New Testament is filled with references to a salvation from death into a new quality of life that begins now through faith (e.g., 1 Peter 1:3f, 'We've been given a brand new life and have everything to live for, including a future in heaven – and the future starts now' [*The Message*]).

Many of the Eastern religions teach that at death the soul leaves the body and then goes back into a great ocean of souls. Or, if it hasn't finished its job of getting all the sin or imperfection cleaned up in this life, it is sent into another body and gets another round of life here on earth. Someone may be reborn as a donkey or a goat or some other person. A person is reincarnated so he or she can finish the spiritual work that didn't get done in this life or however many lives he or she had before. But apparently the soul as understood by Eastern religions is unaware of its past life or lives, and the reincarnated soul does not know it's a donkey, for instance, atoning for its sins.

Most Christians throughout history have believed that after one dies there is a 'resurrection of the body,' that somehow the core personality or identity of the person is intact beyond death. It's a different kind of body, a spiritual identity. Paul gives us a picture of this spiritual body's transformation at death as being like a little brown seed that, after being planted in the earth, comes forth as a huge flower (see 1 Cor. 15). The spiritual body is, like that flower, more than the 'seed' could have imagined.

Jesus said, 'I go to prepare a place for you' (John 14:2). And what I am calling the 'soul' is the inhabiting spiritual center of the body or personality that lives on beyond death. In other words, in the Christian's story there's a place for this spiritual part of our personality – this soul of ours – from now on.

Psychology and the Soul

The second group of writers who have tried to give us a picture of the soul includes psychologists/theologians. Starting with Carl Jung, they have tried to describe the soul with varying degrees of spiritual insight using the language and forms of their own theories. Some random comments give a taste of the views of a few of those studying human behavior and spirituality.

Jung thought of the soul as 'the inner attitude, the character that one displays to his (own) unconscious.' (As opposed to the persona, the mask one displays to the world.)[2] Robert Johnson said, 'My soul is a specific part of me with a specific function . . . The soul of a human being is designed, in a sense, to enable him or her to see a different side of the cosmos, to experience a life and a perspective that is wide and vast. The soul can only do what it is designed to do, what is in its nature: it can only lead us toward the infinite.'[3]

Will Willimon (et al.) have said that 'the search for meaning is primarily concerned with crafting the soul – our only possession that can never be taken away even by death. While we are still alive, our soul is who we are. It is our *being* – our very essence. At the time of our birth, our soul represents the sum of our being . . . the only thing which we have over which we have any control is our soul – not in some mystical, metaphysical sense, but rather in a very practical sense. If there is life after death on the other side of the mountain, we know not how to influence it. But we do know how to influence the condition of our soul, which survives after death, on this side of the mountain.'[4]

Paul Tournier referred to the authentic experiencing center as the 'person,' as opposed to the 'personage' that one shows to the world. He said that the inner person is like a vulnerable child who travels and grows through a field of opposing forces.[5]

Thomas Moore has said many things about the soul: 'It is impossible to define precisely what the soul is. Definition is an intellectual enterprise anyway; the soul prefers to imagine. We know intuitively that soul has to do with genuineness and depth, as when we say that certain music has soul . . . Tradition teaches that soul lies midway between understanding and unconsciousness, and that its instrument is neither the mind nor the body, but imagination . . . fulfilling work, rewarding relationships, personal power, and relief from symptoms are all gifts of the soul . . . We live in a time of deep division, in which mind is separated from body and spirituality is at odds with materialism. But how do we get out of this split? We can't just "think" ourselves through it, because thinking itself is part of the problem. What we need is a way out of dualistic atti-tudes. We need a third possibility, and that third is soul.'[6] And Scott Peck defines the soul as 'A God created, God nurtured, unique, developable, immortal, human spirit.'[7]

The Soul in Action

After looking at both the biblical record and some of the various attempts of psychologists to define the soul, I have come to see the soul as the potential hero of the imperfect cast of an individual's spiritual drama on which we will raise the curtain in the next chapter.

PERSONAL GUIDE AND ADVISER

What comes out of the bulk of the biblical references to the soul seems to be this: there is a special part of us that reflects and draws us toward what is uniquely us in potential. This part focuses our most important spiritual and ethical awareness, and deals with our search for God and with evaluating the reality around us, urging us to integrate with integrity that which appears to be God's will for our lives. Biblical and secular writers seem to agree that without integrity there is ultimately no spiritual journey. Honesty is not the best policy for the soul; it's the only policy.

The soul leads us to who we are designed to be, beneath all our pretensions and masks. It urges us to move toward reality and truth, as appetite urges us toward food. We experience the soul as a living, personal guide and adviser, evaluating everything that comes into our experience. The soul's questions are always, 'What is *real* here? What is of God? What is true, right, and beautiful for us among all the thoughts, actions, people, dreams, and opportunities that come to our attention?'

If God is seen to be ultimate reality, then the soul – the personality's contact point with God – is the part of us that can recognize what is real or true for us and urge us to embrace God. When Mary says, 'My soul doth magnify the Lord,' (Luke 1:46 KJV) I read that to mean that when I praise and express gratitude or love to God, my soul, the part of me that determines what is real and what has integrity, has recognized, focused on, and is embracing and praising the reality that is God.

26

WHISTLE-BLOWER

Besides yearning for and drawing us toward what is real and true from God (Ps. 119:20), the conscience in the soul also sounds the alarm when we attempt to lie, cheat, deceive, or act on anything that is not real or true. The soul, then, is not only the measuring device to determine what is real and right for us, but it contains the *whistle-blowing* conscience to call us back from our tenacious tendency to twist or avoid our own truth and God's, calling us back to be true to our highest values. Moreover, experience indicates that people who follow the nudging of their souls are often very resilient in the face of rejection for doing the right thing, often having the capacity to keep coming back, refreshed, seeking the real and true. They often seem to be willing to face great hardships and come through them, somehow stronger – even after being rejected, ridiculed, or abused for obeying the soul's counsel.

The apostle Paul is a classic example of the paradoxical power and persistence that can come through integrity. As he told the Corinthians:

[More than the rest of you I experienced] far more imprisonments, with countless beatings, and often near death. Five times I have received at the hands of the Jews the forty lashes less one. Three times I have been beaten with rods; once I was stoned. Three times I have been shipwrecked; a night and a day I have been adrift at sea; on frequent journeys, in danger from rivers, danger from robbers, danger from my own people, danger from Gentiles, danger in the city, danger in the wilderness, danger at sea, danger from false brethren; in toil and hardship, through many a sleepless night, in hunger and thirst, often without food, in cold and exposure. And, apart from other things, there is the daily pressure upon me of my anxiety for all the churches . . . [But] I am content with weaknesses, insults, hardships, persecutions, and calamities; for when I am weak, then I am strong. (2 Cor. 11:23–28; 12:10).

It is our soul that guides us to become real, and that yearns for God and His reality and way of persistent integrity.

The Soul's Spiritual Path

The *spiritual* path for the soul is more of a fearful warfare than an educational venture. This inner warfare is very different from much religion. You can be a religious person for years, attending church and participating with your time and money, and never hear or heed this part of your life I am calling the soul. You can be a moral business person or professional, a Christian writer, an ordained minister, a seminary professor, a great evangelist, the pastor of a mega church, or even a bishop and not really be on a spiritual journey guided in any primary sense by your soul. In fact, God sent Jesus right past the numbing religion of the Jewish leaders of His day. He addressed their inner spiritual issues of unreality and separation from God and He confronted them about how their pious, performance-oriented religious lives were not the incarnate spiritual integrity God wanted at all, but merely a behavioral print-out of their inner separation from their souls (e.g., see Matt. 23:23, 29).

According to Jesus, God's remedy for the struggle of His followers to win the inner battle the Pharisees were losing was for Jesus to leave them so that God could send the same loving Personality, the same guiding Spirit they had seen in Jesus to come and dwell *within them* as a resident counselor and strengthener (see John 14:15–17). This personality would inhabit that part of them that was focused on God, that part they called the soul, so that it would not just be a passive repository of the truth of God, but a cleansed residence for the living truth to inhabit. For those who wanted it, the soul, sensitive to the resident Spirit, would be the personal, reality-checking guide to lead the spiritual pilgrim on the adventure of finding the will of God for his or her life. (But we are getting way ahead of our story.)

Let's start at the very beginning of the human spiritual adventure: the birth of a baby.

Almost from its first breath, there is trouble for the child-with-its-soul. It is born into what will turn into a dangerous spiritual war zone, into a seemingly secure life that will soon be inhabited by some very powerful and frightening people and energies, pushing and pulling the baby in different directions.

3

Beginning the Soul's Adventure

IMAGINE THE MOMENT OF BIRTH FROM THE BABY'S perspective.[1] It begins with being squeezed through a constricting tunnel that is like a toothpaste tube, ending (until recent times) with a SLAP! on the bottom by the hand of a giant! Almost simultaneously the baby experiences a sudden chill (another first) and a sunburst of bright lights and shapes in a cavernous room with more giants making loud noises. All this culminates in a complete separation from the warmest and most secure home most people will ever have. If babies were fully conscious and rational, some might surely think they had landed in enemy territory. And some babies do come forth howling in what at least looks like anger.

But evidently when the baby looks out on the world for the first time, the kaleidoscope of colors and shapes is quite meaningless. Until a child learns to give meaning to the shifting shapes and colors, the world at which the baby looks is both fascinating and baffling. Apparently babies begin life unencumbered by conscious meaning and purpose.

Of course, we don't know what actually goes on inside the baby in terms of awareness or the recording of what happens, even in body memories, in the first few hours of life. One thing is certain: the newborn child is in a new world. When compared to the privacy and security of the mother's womb, this new environment is potentially threatening and relatively unstable with regard to meeting all the baby's essential needs.

Because of the baby's experience in the womb, it would seem that the newborn's unconscious expectation might be that this new world will also meet every need and thus provide happiness. Until the traumatic transition of birth, the child's only experience from outside itself was a visceral sensation akin to 'approval' or 'esteem.' But now, in a matter of a few moments, the familiar need-satisfiers of warmth, food, and comfort the child has known are no longer on automatic. Soon the baby's peace will be disturbed even further. For the first time this newborn being will need a new kind of emotional weaponry – knowledge – to win the battle for survival and growth in a world owned and operated by physical giants. The child must learn how to negotiate or manipulate the environment to get his or her needs met. After Otto Rank pointed out the powerful effects of the trauma of birth on a child, it has seemed reasonable to many to connect the painful body memory experienced at birth to the tenacious insecurity and lack of esteem many of us have from childhood.[2] For many, if not most, people there is a feeling, just below the level of consciousness, that we are not going to do well enough in life, that we are going to be deserted and left alone in the world by those most important to us.

The Relationship between Child and Soul

At some point after conception there is a dawn in the life of the child: consciousness, the spiritual matrix for the soul's secret adventure. No one knows exactly when this begins to take place. Whenever consciousness arrives – and eventually sub-consciousness – there is the stirring of identity, an adventuresome personality whose primary traits seem to be self-centeredness and curiosity. After the tumultuous birth experience, the child starts life in the world seeking, in an honest and unanalytical way, to find what's *real* (i.e., useful, friendly, hostile, or tasty) and what's *true* (i.e., dependable to meet the baby's needs and wants) – just what the soul wants to know. In fact, this new child experiences his or her personality as the *same thing as the soul.* They are in harmony while facing the fear and uncertainty of life and trying to determine what's real in their new world. Until the arrival of the awareness that the child can lie and deceive others to get what it wants, there is no conscious ground for inner warfare between the child and the soul about values. Therefore we will postulate in this fantasy that the newborn child is blissfully congruent with his or her reality-checking soul. (For the time being, I will refer to the child as the 'child-soul' – until we see how the separation between the two may occur to set up the first internal battle in the life of the soul.)

To find out what's 'out there,' the child-soul depends on the physical senses: he or she looks at objects, touches them, listens to them, smells them, and tastes them. Because the most constant factors in the baby's life at first are the primary caregivers' presence and ability to meet the infant's basic needs, the baby may focus on the mother and/or father. The baby touches and tastes them.

'Hmm . . . Mommy! Yummy, good!'

'Hmm . . . Daddy! Smells okay but not much in the taste department.'

Over time the baby begins to assimilate experiences, recognize individual people, and postulate the nature of the parents' relation to the baby and his or her needs. He or she soon learns that a smile or 'goo-goo' sound can bring a giant parent, or especially a grandparent, to his or her knees before the baby's bed. At this stage the child-soul is always seeking and storing information about what feels good, what is true, what 'works' and is useful, and what is real.

I remember one shiny spring morning when our youngest child was a baby. A slight breeze from the open window was blowing the ruffled white curtain over her bed. Her head turned as her eye caught the gentle movement. The smell of spring flowers mingled with the scent of baby powder. I was fascinated. I watched her as she lay there quietly checking out her small world. She appeared to study a bright red-and-blue toy suspended just over her face. She would look at it, cock her head, and then reach for it in a jerky baby-lunge manner to try to bring it to her mouth to taste it. Then she turned and saw me. She smiled, and I was suddenly her slave. I smiled too. Later I realized that she was doing the research she would need for her adventure into life beyond the crib.

Apparently this learning is not usually a quiet or thoughtful reasoning experience, but is more like looking into a kaleidoscope that changes shapes and experiences every moment. Recently I was watching a child playing in the park. She fell down, and instantly howled with pain, holding her knee with both hands and looking up at her young mother through saucer-eyed tears. The mother picked up her daughter, held her, and assured her she was okay. Two minutes later the child was back laughing and playing – until she saw a man beating a dog until it cowered in obedience.

Then she was all sadness. She too was doing her research for use later.

As we have seen, the baby's expectations in the beginning might be that its needs will be met in a timely and adequate manner – just as they were in the womb. However, parents are also centered on themselves in some important ways, and many of them never had any training about how to rear children. Therefore the baby's initial expectations are bound to be frustrated and thwarted to some extent. When this happens, the baby starts using the 'tools' with which he or she learned to get food for a different game – power plays.

I remember talking to a friend named Tom. He was telling me about his son Jimmy, a fourteen-month-old who was tyrannizing Tom's family. The child had learned that loud, angry screaming and tears would bring his parents immediately with their checklists of possible messages or requests. Sometimes there was nothing wrong; the child just wanted to avoid his nap or sleeping at night. This behavior was so effective that Jimmy had become a merciless tyrant, keeping the family up far past their bedtime, entertaining Jimmy or holding him late into the night. The family's pediatrician told Tom and his wife to let Jimmy cry the next time they determined that his behavior was just a power play; he would soon get tired of screaming and go to sleep. The next night, however, Jimmy got really angry when Tom wouldn't get him up, and continued screaming almost all night long. He was evidently determined to get control of his parents. Jimmy was unconsciously playing 'war games,' preparing for the battles that were soon to come.

It may well be that the parents' inability to meet all the baby's innocent or impossible expectations engenders fears in the child-soul and leaves the baby with less than the total security it wants, and with less than adequate guidance about how to get along in the world.

Through all this experimenting to get things and people under control in the early beginnings of its life, the child finally realizes that the adult giants are in charge of the goodies in the world. So if the child can't control the adults, it becomes very important – either consciously or unconsciously – to get the caregivers' approval and esteem, not just so the child will be happy, but for physical and emotional survival!

As we shall see, this problem of getting esteem from adults sets up one of the major fears that fuel the inner warfare for survival in the secret life of the soul. This fear of not being in control, and of not winning the esteem of the people who are in control, is not just about children who have been frightened or abused by parents. A client I'll call Joe was raised by a progressive mother (for her time) who gave him her undivided attention and love, and never spanked him. Joe learned almost from the beginning that he could call out, and she would come running to meet his physical and emotional needs. Therefore he should have had happiness and security, and been well adjusted with plenty of self-esteem. But although he seemed to have these things, he did *not*!

Later Joe learned that his mother's compulsive attention to the details of his life was partly to make up for the fact of his father's distance from him – and the father's love and absorption with Joe's older brother, who was a dead ringer for his dad. Very early on Joe felt two things that drove him to fear that he would not get esteem in the world: (1) His mother apparently loved him so much and paid so much more attention to him than Joe's friends' mothers did (to them) that Joe felt like he must be defective somehow or she wouldn't feel she had to pay so much attention to him, help him, and teach him about life so much of the time. (2) Joe's father traveled a great deal in his business and was emotionally absent from Joe – even when he was at home. He almost never had any time to talk or play, and Joe secretly grieved about that. Despite all the attention and love one could ever want from an intelligent and devoted mother, Joe still felt he must not be worth much if his own daddy didn't want to spend time with him.

Over the years I have counseled with people whose fathers were ministers, physicians, psychological counselors, business-men, or in other demanding professions. Many of these children of successful people have grown up to be insecure men and women who have terribly low self-esteem but have become brilliant or successful in their vocational lives.

As an adult counselor, I realized that I was one of these insecure children, trying to win awards from the world – to at least get esteem from strangers, because I too didn't feel I could get love from my father. What's more, in most cases, the people I talked to about this were also hoping to get esteem from a dead parent – love and approval they never felt they got or even deserved when they were children.

The bottom line is that in the experiences of birth and early childhood, virtually every person seems to wind up with a deep fear of not getting enough love and/or esteem. The parents' disapproval of the child's imperfection is perceived by the child as dangerous because the imperfect behavior is not acceptable to the big people who control the distribution of the goodies. Children tend to push the fearful feelings and the lack of self-esteem out of sight into their unconscious. In my case, I have been afraid all my life, yet much of the time I have repressed those fears because of the threat of losing esteem from my father, and later other people, who I thought wanted me to be fearless and courageous.

Long before adolescence, I was so out of touch with my feel-ings that I thought I was just excited when I took an examination, went out for an athletic team, or was considering approaching a girl for any reason. But the truth was that I was afraid, terribly afraid! I often fought intense inner battles to feel good enough about myself and my abilities to try to reach out and try threatening things. Part of me wanted to run away while another part was telling me that I would be worthless if I didn't go through with the test, make the team, or approach the girl.

As a result of these experiences and the failure that often resulted when I tried, I was tempted, as Joe was, to hole up inside and isolate myself from the people and challenges outside myself.

What happens to people who are afraid like this that keeps them from isolating completely and simply not trying to learn what they need for healthy growth and development?

Our Internal Guidance System

At this point a very important question comes up. Is a child-soul totally dependent on the adequacy and maturity of his or her caregivers to learn to reach out for the information, meaning, and direction the child will need to live and develop his or her spiritual and emotional potential? If so, then anyone who has not been given adequate guidance by primary care-givers or who has been abused as a child would no longer hear the guiding voice of his or her soul because of overpowering fear of rejection and abuse. Such a child would lose the chance to discover his or her own truth or reality.

However, there appears to be an amazing internal 'guidance system' made up of longings implanted like spiritual appetites in each child-soul.[3] These 'appetites' nudge us and draw us beyond ourselves in spite of neglect, fear, and lack of self-esteem to find satisfiers to meet specific needs and people essential to us in finding our own particular destiny. Even if a rose were twisted somehow into being a prickly pear cactus plant, it would still at some level long to be a rose. This guidance system also gives us a resilient energy that allows us to keep searching for *our own* truth and a place in life, even after caregivers and others have abused us or tried to control us and twist our wills to accept *their* version of our life as our own. These longings that motivate and guide every child are instrumental in setting the itinerary of the child-soul on its quest for love, esteem, integrity, and God.

But what are these built-in yearnings, and how do they work as a guidance system for the child-soul?

4

God's Guidance System

FROM THE BEGINNING OF THE CHILD-SOUL'S SECRET SEARCH for reality and fulfillment, God has given it a package of 'hints and scents' – or magnetic yearnings – to guide each child in its search. These yearnings draw us beyond ourselves in certain directions out of all those we might choose as we develop physically. The yearnings are experienced as nudges before the child-soul is rational. Just as physical hunger draws us toward food, these yearning-hungers nudge the baby to risk venturing forth to connect with the reality or relationships longed for.

Richard D. Grant Jr and Andrea Wells Miller's book, *Recovering Connections*, describes these as gifts from God;[1] Carl Jung called these built-in longings *archetypes*.[2] Although there are, perhaps, many of these guiding energies, Grant and Miller posit four guidance-yearnings that are extremely useful as we try to understand ourselves. They begin to surface as we start our conscious adventure to find happiness and fulfillment.

Although every child does not develop on the same timetable

or in the same way, these four yearnings usually begin to develop and flower noticeably in the following order:

1. the yearning for perfect parenting: birth to eighteen months;
2. the yearning for perfect companionship: age eighteen months to four years;
3. the yearning for perfect power and freedom: age four to six years;
4. the yearning for perfect meaning: age six years to puberty.[3]

My descriptions will be simplistic, of course, because we can't know exactly what is going on inside a baby, and we realize that much of it is no doubt unconscious. But this idea of built-in yearnings has been very helpful to me as I try to picture what may be some of the early dynamics in the secret inner adventure of a child-soul.

The Yearning for Perfect Parenting

In every child there seems to be a sort of 'image' that appears from within – a mental, semiconscious picture, or sense, of what a perfect parent should be like. We see this image reflected when the child expects that 'somebody' is going to give it the basic things it needs for survival. Very early on, a baby seems to choose one parent or parent figure as the 'main one.' The child quickly fastens onto that parent or other care-giver and almost at once learns how to signal that person in special ways to elicit responses that will get specific needs met.

A friend named Nathan and I were talking about the way kids seem to choose who is for *them* 'the perfect parent.' He shook his head at one point and said, 'One of my daughters learned to use what looked like flirting to get my attention –

while she was just a baby – long before she could have learned these behaviors in the usual way from adults. I remember walking into her room at the end of a nap time. She was lying, relaxed like a rag doll, just waking up when she saw me standing by her bed. She smiled and turned her head away about a quarter turn in a very coquettish manner, her eyes never leaving mine. I laughed, melted, and picked her up.'

Nathan and I both chuckled as he continued, 'Her sister was so different. Her lights came on when her mother came into the room and she hardly seemed to notice me.'

Whatever the signal may be, each child seems to 'select' or bond with one parent or caregiver on whom they focus the yearning for a perfect parent.

When the perfect-parent-yearning is triggered, an energy is evidently released in the child to help that child reach out toward the parent figure. When a baby bonds with a parent, it soon becomes apparent to everyone in the family that there's some kind of special connection between the child and the selected caregiver.

Forming a bond with dependable adults seems to calm the child-soul's fears. When the caregiver comes through in a timely fashion – with food, warm baths, clean clothes, and holding – the little child may feel that 'reality is that there is caring help for me out there.' This secure feeling is very important. Because of the separation trauma at birth, the child-soul has experienced the fact that it can lose the warmest relationship anybody ever had – in the womb of the mother – however unconscious the experience or body-memory might be.

So the yearning and the search for perfect parenting lays an important foundation in the spiritual experience of the child-soul concerning the friendliness or unfriendliness of the world in which it is going to have to live out its adventure. At a deeper level this experiential foundation – or lack of it – foreshadows the possible nature of any future approach to a relationship to God, or avoidance thereof.

The Yearning for Perfect Companionship

As the child-soul develops, a yearning for perfect companionship is triggered. This yearning nudges the child toward other people, first within the family of origin, and then outside of it: friends, and later sweethearts and possible mates. This yearning and the motivational energy it provides are very important to help the child-soul overcome the normal fear of reaching out for new relationships. However, when the yearning is frustrated or the child reaches out and is rejected, the fear can increase and be compounded by shame and feelings of low self-esteem.

I remember one summer when I was about nine years old. Our parents took us on a vacation to Crystal Lake in Michigan. A couple who had been college friends with my mother and father stopped by our cottage for a visit. They had a ten-year-old girl. I had one older brother (who was out fishing with my dad) but no sisters – I knew *nothing* about girls. My mother sent Barbara and me out to 'play together.'

I remembered being very nervous because I had no idea what to say or do. Barbara was beautiful and three or four inches taller than I was. She had long blond hair and clear blue eyes. I thought she was the prettiest thing I'd ever seen, but I was tongue-tied and very uncomfortable. After a few moments of following her around while she kicked clods toward the lake, poked at everything from rocks to trees with a stick she'd picked up, and generally ignored me, she turned to me with a disgusted, superior, and disdaining look. She scrunched up her face as if something smelled bad, and said, 'You don't know how to do *anything*! You're no fun!' She then stalked back to the cabin in contempt and refused to speak to me for the rest of her parents' visit. I felt horrible and shamed, as if I were an idiot child; I refused to come in until they left.

For several years after that experience I concentrated heavily on sports and avoided having anything to do with girls until I was a teenager. The attempt to reach out for perfect companionship can be excruciating.

If it weren't for this yearning, in fact, a child-soul, after a few rejections, might be extremely inhibited about reaching out – or be extremely shy. But the yearning for perfect companionship drives the child, nudged by its soul that is always seeking its reality-destiny, to overcome even great fear and try to enter relationships. The pain and shame of failure in reaching out for perfect relationships might be too much for a child were it not for a strange and unlikely asset: loneliness.

Normal loneliness is the conscious experience of the yearning for perfect companionship. Acute loneliness takes place when this yearning is frustrated or blocked by either exaggerated fear due to real or perceived rejections, or by isolation set up by lack of social opportunities. For years, psychotherapists have said that this intense type of loneliness may be the biggest killer in America.[4] Such fear-filled loneliness can lead people to do harmful things or to enter destructive and/or inappropriate relationships just to alleviate the pain and fear that often accompany such severe lonely feelings. Some of these self-defeating responses to acute loneliness are compulsive or addictive behaviors that can get the lonely person abused, diseased, or killed. Recently, when I was lecturing in Germany about this subject, a woman told me the following story concerning the lengths people can go to avoid being lonely and risking leaving a relationship.

Sammy came from a family that had abused her physically when she was a little girl. She married a man who seemed to love her, but a few months after the marriage her husband changed.

'He became silent,' Sammy said. 'He just quit talking. And when I asked him what was the matter, he would get furious and stare at me with obvious rage. He quit going to church or anywhere and finally stayed home so much he got fired. That was when he started hitting me with his fists when anything I did displeased him. This went on for months.

'I knew I should probably tell someone,' Sammy said, shaking her head, 'but I was too embarrassed about being such a bad wife that my husband beat me. And besides, I had been so lonely when I was single I didn't ever want to be single again. But things got worse. I had to get a job at night to buy food. I didn't do much except work and go to church on Wednesdays – which was my night off.'

Sammy paused and looked at me to see if I was listening. I was listening and nodding, encouraging her to go on if she wanted to. And she did.

'One night I came home late from church and the house was dark, except for the front porch light. I noticed right away that the front door was open – which was a very strange thing for Hank to do. I carefully walked through the open door and started to flip the light on . . . when a hand grabbed my wrist and jerked me forward off my feet. I let out a half yelp of surprise and looked back at the shadowy form in the dark. It was Hank. He had a revolver in his hand – aimed at my face. He carefully closed the door.

'Hank tied me to a straight chair in the bedroom with a cotton rope he had coiled on our bed. He pulled a padded reading chair up behind me. He sat down behind me in the reading chair, and in a monotone voice he told me he was going to kill me when he got ready. He held me hostage all night, only speaking once in a while to tell me what a sorry wife I'd been and to repeat periodically that he was going to kill me. I have never been so afraid. Periodically Hank put the cold gun barrel against my neck. I was terrified and could almost hear my heart pounding. Finally he went to sleep with the gun in his lap. I knew he was asleep because he was snoring. I very carefully wriggled my right wrist free, praying that I would not wake Hank.'

Sammy paused and was silent so long I thought that she wasn't going to tell me what happened. As it turned out, Sammy got loose and went to her parents' apartment 'until the trouble blew over' and she 'could go home.'

Sammy's story is an extreme case; however, *many* people stay in unsatisfactory and even very abusive relationships rather than face the isolation of loneliness again.

Because of the potential for being hurt by those close to us, even in a 'normal' family, it's often scary to the little child-soul (or anyone else) to risk relating personally or intimately. Without the guiding pull of the yearning for perfect companionship and the recurring sense of loneliness, the young child-soul might be too frightened to risk ever being in intimate relationships inside or outside the family.

The Yearning for Perfect Power and Freedom

'I can *do* it *myself*!' Anyone who has raised a small child has probably heard that declaration more than a few times. The yearning for perfect power and freedom has been triggered. At a certain stage of development, the young child-soul longs for the power and freedom to be who he or she is and to do the things he or she thinks of doing when the child wants to do them – instead of only doing what he or she is told. Since the child-soul doesn't know where the boundaries are to its power and freedom, this yearning generates great motivation and energy for the child-soul to test its power and freedom against those people close to it. The 'terrible twos' are about the little soul's early movements toward answering the question, 'How much power and freedom is real for me as a part of this family?'

When I was thinking about how this plays out, I remembered my wife Andrea's mother telling me about what a strong yearning for power and freedom Andrea had as a small child.

'When Andrea was about two years old, she was very active and developed a strong will.' Annelle smiled as she remembered and went on, 'Andrea tested *every* limit she was given. When she was about three, her sister was born and I could not leave the baby and run and catch Andrea when she left the yard to explore. We told her over and over again not to go outside the backyard – but she had kept doing it even though she was punished or grounded. So her father decided that although it was a lot of trouble, he would build a fence around the backyard. He chose a wire fencing that was made up of small squares, and he spent several days building it. When the yard was fenced, I felt a great relief. Andrea was safe.

'But that very same day,' Annelle continued, smiling and shaking her head again, 'Andrea was playing in her sandbox. The telephone rang and I took the baby in and answered it. When I came back out a few minutes later, Andrea was just climbing down the other side of that high fence, fitting the toes of her little sandals into the small squares. She jumped down onto the ground outside the fence as I called to her to stop – and disappeared into a neighbor's yard. She had a really strong need to make a run for freedom.'

I laughed, agreeing that the yearning to test the limits concerning how much power and freedom a child can wrest from her parents can be very strong.

The Yearning for Perfect Meaning

'What's life all about? Is there a God? Why is the world the way it is?' These are the kinds of questions that sooner or later become important to a child experiencing the fourth yearning – the yearning for perfect meaning. This longing gives the soul energy for its long-range search for ultimate reality, for an overall explanation of things – a design that can pull together all a person's experiences, knowledge, and yearnings into a coherent whole that makes sense out of the world and the soul's various kinds of experiences of what is real. It is this implanted yearning for perfect meaning that nudges some people to search for God.

However, an intimate relationship with God does not usually come through academic searching and reading about God (the religious search), but through contact with a person, someone who cares about us and our questions and who seems to be on the same spiritual journey we are.

One year when I was a young teenager, a new teacher, Jim, came to teach the high school class at our church. (We were a bunch of kids who were going through adolescent rebellion but trying to stay out of jail.) Jim was not an athlete, nor was he cool socially. I felt sorry for this new teacher – until he began to talk to us that first Sunday. Some kid on the back row asked him, 'What do you do for a living?'

'I'm a reporter for the newspaper,' he told us. Well, it turned out that Jim was the *crime reporter* for one of the leading newspapers in Tulsa. He was really interested in us, and talked to us about all kinds of real things we brought up. Once we were talking about what happens to criminals who get caught. He told us about the police and court processes. Then he asked us if we would like to talk to some criminals who had been put in prison and see how they felt. We said we would, but we didn't think he could pull that off.

Evidently Jim had connections and was well respected because he took us on a field trip to the state penitentiary. We ate with the prisoners in a huge cafeteria that smelled so much like Clorox that our eyes practically watered. I was very nervous and could imagine being grabbed and held as a hostage. After lunch we took a tour of the prison and ended up walking quietly down death row. I'll never forget that long, dark, concrete tunnel. We saw prisoners there and then went into the execution chamber where a guard explained dramatically, step by step, how the hood went on – and all the details.

On the way home some of us who had been pretty wild during secret parts of our high school careers talked to Jim about God and what he really believed. I confessed to him that I'd been drinking some, and although he didn't drink, Jim never made us feel shamed. Then he left for the Marines as a war correspondent. Later I found out that our quiet young friend had become a war hero. He won a major journalistic prize for his coverage of the battle of Tarawa where he went ashore with the Marines. After the war I wanted to thank him for showing me what God was like, but he'd moved from Tulsa. When I finally got his telephone number, his wife told me he was dead.

I can't remember anything Jim taught us about the Bible or religion. But years later when I decided to try to commit my life to God, I had a living memory of how I might be accepted by God in spite of my sins. My yearning for God had been triggered by a young crime reporter who cared about a bunch of scared, 'show-off' teenagers trying to look cool.

The soul is not so much interested in learning *about* God and religion as it is in being in touch with the reality that *is* God. Just one encounter with a person who loves both God and you the way Jim loved us may provide that sense of contact you can never forget.

Still, there are powerful people and malignant forces that thwart the child-soul's reaching out for fulfillment. And some of these 'enemies' are in our own homes.

5

Static Interference at Home

IN AN IDEAL WORLD, THE INNER YEARNINGS MOTIVATE AND guide the little child-soul to find the reality it needs in a healthy, intimate, loving relationship with parents and significant others inside and outside its family; to develop and claim its own appropriate power and the freedom to exercise it; and to find a close spiritual relationship with God and a personal philosophy based on that relationship.

But there is a problem at this point – a *big* problem! The child is born into a family and a world of imperfect, sinful, and self-centered people with their *own* crying needs, immaturities, and self-serving agendas – sometimes laced with evil. The family's agendas soon conflict with the child-soul's yearnings for a perfect life. So, in the actual imperfect world in which we live, our little child-soul's early adventures responding to the implanted yearnings are met with less-than-perfect responses: inadequate or abusive parenting; painful or rejecting encounters with other people, beginning in childhood; put-downs; and shaming punishment when the child attempts to exercise or test his or her natural power and freedom. And when we search for a perfect meaning to tie life together, we may encounter ridicule, disinterest, denial that there is a God, or insistence on conformity to the tenets of a spiritually deadening religion (e.g., one that focuses inordinately on avoiding mistakes). One or more of these can be used to derail the child-soul's yearning for perfect meaning; that yearning which, if kept intact, could culminate in a longing to *know* God personally, intimately.[1]

When the Yearning Soul is Thwarted

When the family or others in the child-soul's life thwart these basic yearnings, the following are a few of the scenarios that can take place.

THWARTED YEARNING FOR PERFECT PARENTING

When a child reaches out to mother, father, or other caregiver, there are many ways that the parent can thwart that yearning and drive it underground or into distorted relationships.

I once talked with a woman who had become a sex addict. She had three children, two girls and a boy. She favored the boy strongly and flirted with him almost from his birth. She had come to me because her marriage was in trouble after she had several affairs. As she described the men she had gotten involved with, it turned out that they were all older by many years, married, and well established in a business or profession. Most of them appeared to be kind men who listened to her. This had meant so much to her that she 'fell head over heels in love with them.' But when they wanted to break off the affair and go back to their families, she was bereft and very angry.

When I asked her about her parental family, she was silent at first, but then said, 'I loved my father so much when I was a little girl that I jumped on his lap and tried to talk to him the minute he came in the house. He would get very angry with me and tell me to leave him alone, but I just couldn't. Finally he got a long rope and leashed me to the doghouse in our board-fenced backyard. I could only run the length of the rope and back, or get in the doghouse.'

The woman got very quiet. 'I didn't feel good about that, but –' and she paused before continuing with her chin up, '– I still loved my father, and I knew he would change.'

When the yearning for a perfect parent is thwarted in a serious way, the child-soul can get the yearning derailed on all different kinds of searches for the love and self-esteem it never got at home.

THWARTED YEARNING FOR PERFECT COMPANIONSHIP

There are all kinds of ways the yearning for perfect companionship can be stifled, blocked, or distorted. For example, a little girl may have been very shy or been in a family that moved a lot. For whatever reason, she didn't relate to other children. She may have grown up looking very normal – a quiet, intelligent woman. But when she marries, if she doesn't find her husband to be the perfect companion she dreamed of, unusual things can happen.

A woman named Jill complained to me that her teenage son, K. R., had been a 'perfect child' until his junior year in high school. Then he just disappeared emotionally and stayed away from home as much as possible. 'We have always been very close and affectionate,' she said, 'and all of a sudden he doesn't want anything to do with me.'

At first I thought this was just normal adolescent rebellion, but as Jill described their relationship, I saw that the problem was something deeper. She had made K. R. 'her little man.' She had told him all her secrets and even taken him to church and to the city's opera series with her because her husband wouldn't go. She had dressed him up and taught him to hold the door for her and shake hands firmly with men or women she introduced him to. The father had become even more distant from the son and his wife and showed signs of being angry with the boy 'over nothing.' Before long I realized that except for overt sex, Jill had made K. R. into her lover/companion. Eventually Jill was able to see that she had reversed the parent/child role and was using her child. She had been training him to be the perfect companion she'd always longed for and never had, to get the love and esteem she had not received from friends or her husband. Yet in the process of getting these things from her son she had thwarted his yearning for a perfect parent and robbed him of much of his childhood.

K. R. felt a mass of guilt about some of his feelings for his mother. He had learned from her to be afraid of strong women, and yet was drawn to them. Inside, his little child-soul was very insecure and anxious as he tried to fill a grown man's shoes while still only a little boy. K. R. was having to parent his own parent, and he had a great deal of trouble relating to either girls or boys his own age.

There are many other ways a child can be emotionally, physically, sexually, or spiritually abused that block the yearning for perfect companionship in his or her life and the natural development of the child-soul. These harmful experiences create and intensify the fears and inner warfare which make up much of the soul's secret adventure.

THWARTED YEARNINGS FOR
PERFECT POWER AND FREEDOM

Jack and Henry were brothers. Jack was six years older than Henry and teased him mercilessly, calling him 'sissy' or 'panty-waist' at every opportunity. Their father prided himself on being a 'man's man' and encouraged Jack's teasing by smiling at it when it happened. Then the boys' yearning for perfect power and freedom surfaced. When their father punished them for their experiments with independence, the boys reacted in almost opposite ways. Jack took any physical abuse as a lesson on how he could use it on others and became physical toward Henry. Henry, however, felt the injustice of the punishment from the father and became afraid of conflict – especially physical conflict.

When they grew up, Jack became an outstanding football player, very physical with opponents. Henry became known for being very smart, and made excellent grades. He was 'super sweet' to everyone and never offended anyone openly, yet he used his power passive-aggressively, by making cutting, sarcastic – or veiled shaming – comments about others' imper-fections. When people got angry about his veiled passive-aggressive attacks, Henry would shame them further by looking innocent and saying, 'What's the matter with you? Can't you take a *joke*? I was only *teasing*!' (He was like the proverbial St Bernard dog who would wag his tail, jump up, put his paws on people's shoulders, and lick them on the face, while wetting on their shoes.)

When the legitimate yearnings in children for perfect power and freedom are squelched by physical or emotional punish-ment or ridicule, the energy connected to the yearnings can be diverted to create different kinds of powerful and abusive personalities. Although such people as adults may appear to be strong, many are very fearful and miserable inside.

THWARTED YEARNINGS FOR PERFECT MEANING

Sometimes people make lifetime vocational choices and succeed, only to wind up unhappy – even when the 'choice' would appear to be positive or even noble.

Sam was a respected parish minister. When he was a young boy he asked his parents all kinds of questions about life – particularly about God. But Sam was not happy when he came up to me. In our first conversation Sam said, 'My mother made fun of ministers and would have nothing to do with the church. She always said, "Ask your father," when I asked her a question about God. Once Mother looked up from her paper when I was leaving for church with my aunt and said, "Just remember to keep your hand on your wallet around preachers."'

'So how did you get in the ministry?' I asked Sam.

He thought a minute and said, 'When I was growing up, two very fine Christians at different times took my questions about God seriously and spent a lot of time talking to me. One was a Sunday school teacher and the other was a camp counselor. They were positive, cared about me, and made a lot more sense than Mother.'

'How did your mother feel about these men?' I asked.

'She hated them. She said they were both "probably homosexual," spending all that time with young boys. And she forbade me to be with them – but I went to see them anyway. And I became a Christian, and later a minister.'

'Do you think your becoming a minister had anything to do with your mother?'

Sam started to laugh. 'Good gosh, no—' he started to say, but then stopped in the middle of the sentence and stared past me out the window at nothing for a few seconds. Then he looked at me and said, 'I never saw it then, but I think I became a minister and have been hard on Christians who were not being authentic to prove to my mother that God is real and Christians are good people.'

However the misdirection, denial, or distortion of one's yearnings takes place, the resulting fear and confusion, and the energy behind the thwarted yearning, can drive the child, and later the adult/child, to give up the adventure of its own soul to find reality and get the searcher trapped in inappropriate vocations, unreal and controlling behaviors, relationships, and goals that don't lead to reality and peace but to shame, failure, separation, and unhappiness. In many people's lives, behaviors or vocations that are not based on reality – that is, not related to one's basic conscious or unconscious dreams and aptitudes – set up anxiety and inner conflict because of the soul's insistence on the child 'doing the real thing.' This anxious state can be very painful, even if the thwarted dreams or aptitudes are not conscious to the one denying them. Baffling inner warfare and the tragedies of the secret life of the soul can result.

Now we are ready to look at the way an individual may *experience* – in a self-conscious way – the inner warfare and separation that result from the child-soul's encounter with the imperfection and abuse of those in its personal world.

6

The Soul's Battle is Joined

DURING THE CHILD-SOUL'S SURVEY OF HIS OR HER POSTNATAL world, the infant has inspected everything within the ever expanding reach of his or her senses. The four basic yearnings have guided and focused the search, but in that reaching forth, the baby has had only partial success, along with rejection and various kinds of abuse. Inside, these failures create fear, lack of self-confidence, and lack of self-esteem.

After a few years we see a big change in the child-soul's spiritual search for reality. Although many of the experiences discussed so far were no doubt unconscious to the child-soul, there comes a time when some children are aware in a self-conscious way that they are on a spiritual journey – or at least that God is a reality that is something like a person, a reality that can interact with them in a frightening or threatening way, or can offer unexpected help and comfort. Even a simple encounter with God as being real can change forever the way the child-soul views the world and make him or her aware that there is much more out there than he or she had imagined.

The earliest experience of self-conscious spiritual contact evidently comes at different times and in unique ways for different people according to how spiritual one's parents and other caregivers are. For me, this happened when I was a little boy.

I was almost five years old. My bedroom was dark. The only light was a thin yellow-white shaft cutting through the crack from the almost-closed door into the upstairs hall. My mother was sitting on the side of the bed, her hand touching my head on the pillow. She was saying a bedtime prayer. Her words were soothing and familiar as she ended the prayer with, 'In Jesus' name we pray, Amen.'

I had always loved those quiet moments. All day long I had to act tough and strong so my dad and older brother wouldn't think I was a sissy. But during those few minutes alone with mother each night, I could relax in the bed and be what I was – a tired little boy.

Just as she was leaving, she looked at me thoughtfully and sat back down.

'Johnny,' she said, 'it's time you began praying. God is listening for you to talk to Him – just like I do.'

I didn't know what to say. I loved listening to her voice as she said prayers, but I hadn't thought about what her praying implied concerning the *reality* of God. I suddenly felt anxious and totally awake.

'You mean God's actually listening for *me* to say something?'

She raised her eyebrows and nodded her head.

I squeaked a loud whisper, 'You mean he's right here in this room?'

'Yes,' she said, smiling, 'and He's forgiven you for all your sins, and loves you very much.' She leaned down, kissed me on the forehead, and left, closing the door.

When I heard her footsteps going down the stairs, I pulled the covers up to my eyes and peered into the blackness. I was really frightened. Somehow I located what I thought was God up in the left-hand corner of the room. My heart was beating faster. I thought of all the things I had said, and thought, and done in that room alone with the door closed – things I would *not* want God to know about. I was afraid God could hear my heart beating.

I couldn't say anything, and I stayed awake until I could hardly keep my eyes open – so God wouldn't do anything surprising. Then, just as I thought I was going to have to call out in fear (and mortify myself), I remembered that my wise, earthy mother had said, 'God has *forgiven you* for all your sins – and He *loves you* very much.'

I thought about that a few minutes.

As I was dropping off to sleep, I whispered my soul's first conscious prayer: 'Thank you, God.'

My spiritual journey had begun.

Saying that prayer was very different from listening to my mother say prayers. It was my child-soul's first conscious *spiritual* experience. It wasn't just some people at church singing and calmly saying religious words about God, or other people reading and talking about religious ideas. All of a sudden somebody *big* and *powerful* was in my own room and wanted to talk with *me*! This was exciting and dangerous.

That's where the power of a spiritual awareness first awakens – as we change from dealing with ideas we think or hear *about* God to somehow *experiencing directly* a living presence. Whenever or however it takes place, this change is what happens to people who become spiritually alive.

Remember, the little child-soul is an information-gathering system, trying to get 'the facts' about what is true so it can be real and find its identity and purpose. Whenever or however the child-soul experiences God as a reality – like the reality of a parent, or of food, or a house – then that child's inner adventure can take on a new and enhanced awareness as it continues to check out the world around it.

When I was a small boy my grandmother died, and her open coffin was in our living room. My mother could see that I was frightened by death. She put her hand on my shoulder as I stood looking in the coffin of my too-white-and-powdery grandmother. Mother said, 'God is here, Johnny, so everything will be all right.' Those words and her faith that they were true made their way beyond my fears into my soul, which verified the truth so clearly that I relaxed and felt what I was convinced was God's presence in that room.

The Advent of Fear and Shame

There is a *lot* of fear involved in the child-soul's search for what is true and what will work in life. When we misdiagnose a situation as small children, and act on our misdiagnosis, we are sometimes punished or shouted at. For example, a baby boy's parents may act happy and pleased when he throws a ball. They encourage him to do it again and again, rewarding him with 'good boy' strokes. So one day the baby gets hold of a fine china cup, an heirloom – looks like a ball to him – and throws it from his high chair to an oak floor, and it shatters. The baby may get punished or the mother may scream, '*Shame* on you!' Parents are human and they punish children for such 'throwing,' to keep them from repeating the part about the china.

I think many parents hated it when they were shamed as children, but they still use shame to discipline their own kids, not because they mean to hurt them, but because it often works. And so we pass on this shame from generation to generation – 'the sins of the fathers' – although this shaming is often unconscious.

Sometimes harried parents shout not from anger but from sheer frustration and overload. I remember an incident at our house when our kids were little. We had a Kiddie Koop baby bed for our children, a wonderful innovation, invented, I think, more than 70 years ago. There were screen panels on the sides and folding screen panels on the top. You could put this baby bed outside in the backyard in warm weather, put the baby on the mattress, and be assured that the mosquitoes wouldn't get in. Our Kiddie Koop was an attractive antique as I recall, with all of the screen wire painted white.

One afternoon I put our daughter in the Kiddie Koop for her nap. She was just able to stand up and was a very active child. This particular day she evidently was not sleepy and had gotten an artistic urge. The only 'medium' she could employ was suddenly provided for her when her laden diaper came undone and the contents rolled out onto the mattress. Taking her time, she covered much of the screen on three panels, then she curled up and went to sleep while her artwork dried.

Have you ever tried to get that out of a screen? You couldn't do it with a fire hose! (Actually part of the cleaning had to be done with a toothpick.)

As her harried father, who had the nap duty for three daughters that day, I discovered her triptych art production. I saw the deed, and before I could stop myself I shouted, 'No! Shame on you!' She woke up crying and no doubt shocked, and when I looked up, I saw this little angel, her face, hands, and arms covered with her 'medium,' standing there crying big tears and holding her arms out toward me.

I picked her up and we both collapsed on the floor laughing. But was the too-loud, harried shout – or others like it – already registered within her?

To the little child-soul, a punishment may feel like the withdrawal of love and esteem, especially when parents shout at a child. Now I don't care if the parent is St Angelica or a great minister; he or she has probably shouted at his or her children at home when no one is around. When I was too tired, hungry, lonely, or angry, I was even more likely to shout at our children. Only recently I quit shaming my kids that way when I am angry because they won't put up with it any longer. (It's no wonder, they are all past age 35!) But the bottom-line message that a child-soul often receives (and that is recorded inside for a long time – perhaps life) when shouted at is, 'If I'm not doing it right, I'm a *bad person*!'

Shaming Miscommunications

The sad thing from the parents' perspective is that shaming messages may not have seemed abusive at all to the people originally delivering them; yet the content received and recorded by the child was whatever he or she *thought* the care-givers were saying.

Kids are notorious for misunderstanding messages of all kinds this way. Pat Mellody tells a story about a father who loved his son, Wil, very much. When Wil went to the first grade his father almost went with him. After about three weeks Wil came home from school one day crying. The father was very upset and held Wil, asking him, 'What's the matter, son? What happened?'

Wil replied through his tears, 'It's my teacher. She called me a bad name in front of the class – and made me sit in the corner.'

The father was now on red alert. 'What did she call you, Wil?'

'A scurvy elephant!' And Wil sobbed.

'A SCURVY ELEPHANT?' Wil's father was furious! He looked at his watch, realizing he just might catch the teacher before she left that day. He took Wil with him back to the school and classroom.

The teacher looked up from her desk and smiled. Wil's father was not smiling. He said in clipped words, 'I understand you called my son a bad name in front of the whole class.'

'A bad name?' The teacher asked, very surprised. 'What bad name?'

'He reported that you said he was a scurvy elephant.'

'What?' she said, thinking back to the incident. Then she smiled slightly and held up her hand – palm toward Wil's dad – as she said, 'Oh no. I said he was a "disturbing element." I'm sorry.' It's obvious that the child's perception doesn't even have to be accurate for a critical message to be shameful and very painful in the child's life.

Sadly it is true that many children have been severely abused by their parents. But it is also true that many people think they have been abused as children when they had fairly normal parenting by well-meaning parents who were not in touch with the effects of their behavior or with their own (or their children's) souls.

Internalized Shame

When parental shouting or punishing continues, shaming, condemning voices take up residence inside us and continue to attack our self-esteem.

These critical voices have always – up to this point – been outside the child but aimed at correcting him or her. But very soon in life the voices move *inside* the child-soul's mind where they continue to critique the child's thoughts and behaviors.

After that, when the child starts to do something questionable that he or she thinks might displease the parents, the *inner* voices say things like, 'No! *No*! You're stupid! You shouldn't even *think* like that! *Shame* on you!' The child may be all alone when this happens, but the outer shaming voices of parents or caregivers have now been implanted within the mind of the child and are digging in for a lifelong battle. Although the parents' anger, sarcasm, and power were temporary, those of the voices may be continuing and almost constant from then on. After this the parents don't have to shout as much. Their critical shaming voices may ride inside the child for the rest of its life – unless the individual is freed from them later on.

An amazing thing about these voices is that they go far beyond just repeating shaming phrases to the child-soul. They seem to develop into an inner shaming *personality or personalities* who appear to act creatively on their own to shame us for any imperfections and to try to stamp out any self-esteem. This may be a little of what the reported experiences of personal evil are about. For example, I can remember that even when I made a high grade on an examination in high school, and my parents were pleased, the inner shaming voices laughed about the 'dumb things I missed,' and said to me, 'What an idiot! You *should* have made a hundred!' The high grade was spoiled, and I felt shame instead of elation. Such messages are irrational and often relentless. These shaming inner voices, originally planted as introjected messages – childhood impressions of being ignored, belittled, or shamed by parents or early caregivers – may secretly dominate the inner life of even very successful and otherwise well-adjusted adults.

Learning Secrecy

As these voices are becoming part of the child's inner world, he or she has an additional problem. A little boy, for instance, thinks Mom and Dad can read minds. He thinks for a while that the parents know everything about him. After all, out of the clear blue sky Mom says, 'You have to potty' and she's right every time. Of course, the child is not aware that he is sending out a few signals like squirming, hopping, and clutching himself. The small child just believes that Mom or Dad knows everything he is thinking.

This delusion of parental omniscience on the part of children leaves them no place to hide. This time of life therefore may be particularly difficult and fearful for a little child as he or she tries to check life out and get acceptance and love.

But then an amazing thing happens at some time in the little child-soul's adventure. We don't know the exact age for every child, but it's usually in the first few years. A realization comes that provides a way out of being quite so vulnerable, a way to live more comfortably with all the powerful exterior and interior controlling voices.

Let's look at a 'home video' scenario of a little boy named Billy, on Easter Sunday morning. It's been raining for two days and nights but is now bright and clear. Billy's mother had dressed him in his new white Easter clothes. He begs, 'Can I go outside?'

With some hesitation, because of Billy's poor record in the keeping clean department, she sends him outside to wait for the rest of the family. Her final instruction to him is, 'Don't get dirty! Stay out of the mud!'

Soon Billy is standing right on the edge of the concrete driveway, looking at his reflection in a big, wonderful, almost black mud puddle beside the slab. Billy wants to get into that mud so much he can hardly stand it. Just as he is about to stick his hand in the mud, the neighbor kid, Bobby, comes out – also dressed in a new white Easter suit.

Billy looks up, sees Bobby and says, 'Come here; I want to show you something.' The other boy comes over and Billy tells him, 'Bend over here and look. You can see yourself!' When the neighbor boy bends over to see his reflection, Billy can't resist. He pushes Bobby on his face in the mud puddle. Bobby comes out of the mud howling, dripping black muddy water, and furious. Just at that instant both mothers come out.

The mother of Billy, the perpetrator, asks, 'Did you push Bobby in the mud?' Her voice has a *very* angry tone that frightens Billy. He knows she has a real thing about violence – unless she's doing it.

Up to now Billy has never lied because he thinks his mother can read his mind. But all of a sudden under the pressure of the impending punishment, he decides to lie, knowing he's going to get whopped anyway.

And so he says, 'No, no, no, I didn't touch Bobby. He slipped and fell all by himself – on that rock,' and he points to a large flat rock next to the mud puddle.

She stares hard at him, but he doesn't flinch. And, miracle of miracles, Billy's mother *believes* him! And says evenly to Bobby's mother, 'My boy didn't push Bobby!' And she drags him toward the car.

Billy is astounded! 'Good gosh,' he thinks. 'She can't read my mind!'

Look at the *possibilities*! Now he can live *two* lives. He can live one life on the outside that other people can see, and another secret life inside, where people won't know what he's thinking unless he tells them! He is seeing the possibilities of Sin and feeling its seducing power!

Paul Tournier says this ability to keep a secret is a crucial point in the formation of a mature human personality, the first movement of the child toward morality.[2] We can't be moral until we can make decisions in secret, privately, about doing or not doing things that reflect our moral values.

But back to Easter Sunday. When Billy lies that morning (or whenever it happened first), Billy's *soul* is shocked! At that moment an internal division forms between the child and the soul as the soul realizes, 'This lad and I are *not* on the same adventure!' The soul calls out to Billy, 'No, lying is *not* acceptable!'

At this point our little boy has instigated unreality or lack of integrity into his experience by telling the lie. From then on, the child-soul's battle around issues of integrity escalates. Not only does the child have to fight the exaggerated – and thus unreal – shaming voices when they put down the child's attempts to gain self-esteem, but now the child has to fight the soul too. The child's newly discovered defense of lying can put all kinds of dishonest and untrue thoughts and behaviors into action that trigger the soul's conscience function and hinder the soul's task of leading the child to reality and to self-esteem through the process of living with integrity. This can be confusing for the soul, too, because it is a part of the child's experience, influenced acutely by the imperfect and sinful behavior of the rebellious and suddenly dishonest child's personality. When the child perceives a certain amount of freedom from authority by being dishonest, the child may subtly shift his or her self and self-centered desires along with the tool of lying or devious manipulation into the center of the child's focus, replacing the curiosity about life and the world around him or her. This shift is a classic picture of Sin (putting one's self in the center where only God [reality] is properly in place). The unhealthy and destructive temptations of the will often begin to influence the child *from within*, urging the child to ignore what others want and to be captain of his or her own soul. Now a serious and sometimes daily inner conflict can begin. The former friendship and sense of oneness of the child with the reality-oriented soul changes drastically.

Now when the child does or says something dishonest, the soul blows the whistle on that unreality and says, 'Tweeeeeeeet! You're not being honest! Admit it and make amends!'

At the same time the shaming voices tune up and scream at the child, '*Shame* on you! They'll see that you are a phony!' So the interior warfare escalates acutely because of the lying. Both the soul and the shaming voices are accusing the child – the soul for the *immorality* of the lie, and the shaming voices for *being revealed and shamed as not being perfect*.

This new conflict is interior and unseen, because now other people don't know whether the child is not being honest or real unless he or she confesses it or gives the dishonesty away through guilty facial expressions. This child is learning to lie (and learning to act as if he or she is *not* lying) to keep from being shamed and rejected by those whose esteem the child seeks in the world. He or she is also being made to feel *guilty* for the value transgression of lying, or the deed the lying is covering, by the whistle-blowing soul. The combination of shame and guilt can be excruciating.[3]

At this point the child could (and in some cases does) choose to confess, and he or she might discover the esteem rewards for that. Or the child could refrain from confessing but decide not to lie again. This sort of adjusting is part of the normal socialization process everyone goes through. However, in the drama I am presenting about the secret life of the soul, because of internal pressures – the power of the shaming voices and the fear of rejection – many children make a very different choice than that of confession or committing never to lie again.

The child sees a way to avoid some of the pain and conflict caused by the two very vocal critical interior forces in his or her life that are experienced consciously and often. One force is the soul with its insistence on *reality* and *integrity*. The other critical force consists of the shaming voices' condemnation for any imperfection, and their implicit demands for perfect success. The child, very frightened about the possibility of being revealed and rejected, begins to take certain self-defensive steps toward defeating these now defined enemies.

The child doesn't know that he or she has embarked on a course that will lead to an almost complete change in his or her life and goals, but as the decision that I am about to describe is made, a tragedy of major proportions is on the horizon for the soul.

7

Building a 'Constructed Personality'

THE REALIZATION THAT WE HAVE A PRIVATE INNER LIFE AND that we can lie provides the possibility of a whole different strategy and game plan. The child feels trapped by fear. On one hand the shaming voices threaten to reveal the child as being imperfect, dishonest, and bad. To make matters worse, the soul demands that the child face and admit her or his failures honestly – even if it means punishment, rejection, or failure. The apparently universal 'decision' to act drastically at this point to defend ourselves and get approval may be conscious to some. However, what I am about to describe is usually *unconscious* and happens gradually in consequence of several painful experiments in lying, in which the child wrestles with his or her soul but in the end ignores its entreaties and tells lies again – and again.[1]

This struggle is also influenced if the child knows that a parent is lying and uses the parent's dishonesty to justify his or her own falsehood. I remember as a small boy hearing my mother – whom we all knew was very honest in her dealings with people – tell a woman on the telephone, 'Oh, thank you. I'd love to come to your party, but I have to take my son, Keith, for a checkup at the doctor's that day.' I remember being confused and thinking, '*I just went for my checkup yesterday.*' When I reminded her of that, she was irritated and a little flustered, but said, 'Well, it's too late now. I've already said no!'

The balance of the child's decision about his or her integrity in the future is tipped against the soul by the fact that the shaming voices' fear-provoking warning to avoid failure and shame is often louder and more insistent than the soul's quieter – seeming naive – entreaties. In order to avoid the shame of the condemning voices that continually bombarded the child with the message that he or she is inadequate and not worth much, the child begins to look for a more permanent way out and does a very strange and ingenious thing: The child *begins secretly to construct another personality*, one that is false but appears to be more adequate, intelligent, and/or honest than the child actually is.

An example of how this can begin was told to me by a young woman I'll call Janice:

As a small girl I wanted to be loved by my father, but my father seemed to love my two older brothers more than me. He ignored me when he came home from work but played catch with them and taught them how to excel at all kinds of sports that in those days were 'boy sports.' My brothers called me a sissy and 'just a no-good girl.' I cried and secretly felt ashamed of being a girl. So at some point I must have decided to be as nearly a boy as I could be, to get my father's attention and avoid being shamed by my brothers.

I tried always to dress like a boy in jeans and boy's shirts. I begged until I got a boy-like haircut. I remember that I tried to roller skate like my brothers did, and practiced that kind of cool swagger-skate the way they did, shifting my weight easily from one side to the other and surveying the terrain, paying no attention at all to my feet. When I rode my small bicycle, I loosened my shirt tail so my shirt would billow out in the back – like boys' did. I even learned to swear and make nasty signs before I could understand the meanings of what I was communicating.

In short, I began to build and live out the life of a tomboy, although years later I discovered that underneath it all I am very feminine and like being a woman.

Of course this construction of a false personality really pushes the buttons of the whistle-blowing soul. Remember, the soul's nature is to believe that reality and integrity are the only things that can lead to spiritual maturity and the gift of authentic self-esteem.

Construction Begins

As this construction of a false personality begins to happen,[2] the soul screams at the child, 'No! This is *not* the way of reality for you!' It screams so loudly, in fact, that the child makes a drastic – though usually unconscious – decision that will change the entire course of the individual's life. This decision can derail the secret adventure of the child (as well as the soul) from its search for reality, integrity, and God – perhaps forever. This happens when the pain and anguish of the child has increased dramatically as the child is caught in the middle of the escalating warfare between the unreal constructed personality fighting off these shaming voices and the now screaming, pleading soul.[3]

The escalation increases until the child, in a drastic move to avoid the pain of the inner struggle, *separates itself from the soul* and locks the soul in a dungeon within his or her unconscious mind to quiet its screaming insistence that the child strive with all it has for reality and integrity, for congruence – what the soul considers to be the only roads to fulfillment and peace. The soul of such a child is sent down deep in a prison of denial. And our boy in the 'home video' moves away from his now imprisoned soul, because the soul has threatened to get him to reveal his dishonesty and the unreality of the new life he is constructing.

From a practical standpoint, denial isn't *perfect* in its ability to keep the soul's entreaties and whistle-blowing out of consciousness. Yet even when the soul's voice is heard, it is often dimmed by the walls of the prison and drowned out by the urging of Sin and the luring visualizations of evil. The muted whistle-blower can often be overridden without the former excruciating struggle.

The shaming voices' threats to the child of revealing his or her shameful nature as 'a liar' have convinced the child that going public and confessing any serious imperfection is unthinkable.[4]

Although it is appropriate to have some secrets and privacy, the child doesn't know how much is okay. The shaming voices may accuse the child of being a coward for keeping perfectly legitimate secrets. Therefore the construction of a personality that *appears* to be honest (and is in denial about any dishonesty) seems like the perfect out. One doesn't have to confess if one can't *see* any wrong-doing.

At some level the child hates this falseness and the sense of separation it brings, but believes he or she needs the secrecy and dishonesty to succeed in getting esteem and happiness. The first step in constructing a new adequate-looking personality is locking up the soul. When the meddling soul has been put in isolation – imprisoned – the child has laid the cornerstone for the construction of the larger, 'more-righteous (stronger or intelligent) -than-life' but false, 'constructed personality' that he or she hopes will perform adequately enough to quiet the shaming voices. And the habit of denial (*unconsciously* hiding from one's self, as well as others, anything that might reveal his or her dishonesty or unreality) has been established.

Much of this transformation is an unconscious process, although one may be conscious of making certain changes to fit the unconscious construction. Many people have told me that as children they secretly studied more than they said they did – not to gain knowledge but to appear to be smart. The child is usually aware only that being constantly accused of being bad or 'not enough' is extremely painful. So, consciously or unconsciously, he or she begins to construct this false personality that has the soul locked inside it. Then the child can be dishonest if necessary in order to continue to construct, polish, and present anywhere this larger, more important, smarter-looking personality.

Making the Switch

The purpose of the constructed personality is twofold. The first is to quiet the shaming voices. After all, in our constructed person we are now *looking* and *acting* more intelligent, cool, tough, sexy – whatever the shaming voices have told us we are not.

The second purpose of the constructed personality is to

represent to the world inflated constructed characteristics in order to succeed 'out there.' Many of us feel we must succeed or at least look successful and strong in order to earn the esteem from others that we do not feel inside. Therefore we start acquiring adequate-appearing traits, habits, and possessions to hide any signs of weakness or imperfection.

People build very different-looking constructed personalities. Instead of building a larger/smarter personality, some people establish a 'victim'-constructed personality that accepts the blame for everything – even sometimes when it wasn't the person's fault – in order to keep peace and avoid the pain of confrontation. At a deep level both the brash offender and the victim-constructed personalities have the same problem. Both have constructed unreal or false personalities to try to get love or esteem. Both parties can be equally separated from their souls. Neither can dare to share their underlying lack of self-acceptance, so neither can be authentically intimate. Both, in fact, have the same problem, but one hides personal weakness and fear of inadequacy behind a constructed face of strength, while the other hides the *same* fear of inadequacy behind a facade of weakness or even ineptitude, running from success in order to avoid the pain of other people's jealousy or resentment because of that success. Paul Tournier said that everyone makes the choice to appear strong or weak to better negotiate his or her particular circumstances.[5]

I remember a devastating encounter that took me completely by surprise when I was a young boy about ten years old – an encounter that added an element to my constructed personality that still affects my life. A boy I'd met at church came by our house to see me late one summer afternoon. I was a thin kid in a growth spurt, and I was dressed only in a pair of play shorts. When I came to the door, the boy seemed to be shocked as he looked me up and down and said, 'My gosh, when I saw you at church in your suit I thought you had a good build.' He laughed derisively and shook his head as he delivered the life-changing blow, 'But you're just a skinny kid with *no muscles at all.*' And he, being a well-built boy, turned and rode away on his bicycle. I was totally surprised and felt overwhelming shame about my skinny body.

Although I never told anyone about that interchange, I began doing pushups and even, over a period of several years, lifted weights so I could be a 'masculine-looking' hero-type person. This became the physical part of my constructed personality. From the time of that brief encounter I never *felt* that I *was* an attractive male, but at least I wanted to *look* like one. Therefore I've always worked hard at watching my weight and exercising my body. I kept it up in spite of the fact that for years I was told I was nice looking and even wound up being elected 'king' of a high school of thirty-five hundred kids.

The shaming voices inside tell us that we don't deserve to feel self-esteem without looking or performing *outstandingly*, so we construct a personality absolutely focused on succeeding. The hope is that when we have succeeded unmistakably, our shaming voices will at last say, 'Good boy!' or 'Good girl! You have at last done it right! And we love you!' At *that* point, we hope to finally feel good about ourselves, to finally have *self*-esteem.

For these outcomes to occur, a transformation of intention is required. In the beginning the child-soul's joint focus was on the search for *reality:* 'What's real here, and what does it taste like? Feel like? How does it work? What do I do with it? Eat it? Throw it on the floor, etc?' But when the child locks up the soul and begins to build a constructed personality, the focus of the child's life is no longer to find out what's *real*, but to discover what will bring the child *success* and *esteem* in all things. This is achieved through the constructed personality's strong posture and compulsive drive for success – regardless of what's real from the soul's perspective.

As I suggested earlier, although my constructed personality was built to respond to shame voices that told me I was not strong enough, not successful enough – not *male* enough – many women (and men) build their constructed personalities to counteract shaming voices that say they are too assertive, too strong, too talented – not *female* or *gentle* enough. Although I will continue to describe my own super adequate, success-driven constructed personality, the reader may see the same dynamics and struggles regarding his or her own very different-looking construction.

The choice of a vocation is often made by the constructed personality – not to fulfil the soul's yearning or a natural apti-tude, but because a child sees in that particular vocation a chance to find the self-esteem he or she doesn't feel inside since his shaming voices have told him he is not worthy. Burt is an example. As an adult he told his counselor that he had been a rebellious child and got in trouble everywhere he went. He was so anti-social and belligerent to other kids, even as a three-year-old, that the nursery at church wouldn't keep him during adult worship service.

His parents, who were serious Christians, had to take Burt into the 11:00 church service with them. They seated him between them so they could control him more easily as they listened to the sermon. Burt said, 'One Sunday I had drawn pictures all over the program and was looking around trying not to go nuts from boredom while waiting for the sermon to be over. Suddenly the preacher made a dramatic point and there was a hush in the room.' Although Burt knew that he would no doubt be punished for what he was about to do, he couldn't resist. In a clear, resonant, three-year-old-voice, Burt said, 'AMEN!'

Several things happened in the next few seconds that had never happened to Burt. All eyes turned and looked at him, but this time people were smiling! To his amazement, his mother had a look of pleased wonder and surprise on her face (instead of the rejection he had feared) as she whispered to his father, 'Did you hear that? Little Burt said "Amen!"' His father nodded, smiled, and patted Burt on the back.

'In that instant,' Burt said to me, smiling wryly, 'a minister was born!'

Burt said that from then on he was asked to 'say the blessing' at mealtime and later to help in the Sunday school. He began to realize that he could get the love and esteem for which he was starved by praying and saying religious things. When Burt prayed, magic took place: his father loved him and his mother was ecstatic! He later went to seminary and eventually became the minister of a large church. But then, before he was 40, Burt was burned out and went to counseling. After telling his story, he said thoughtfully, 'I wasn't called by God to the ministry – I was sent by my mother.'

Whether this story is told by a minister, a teacher, a banker, or a pro football player, the burnout can be the same. They eventually realize that what they are doing is not connected with who they *really* are in their souls, but rather is a part of a more or less unreal life they have constructed to get the success and approval that was supposed to give them the esteem – and self-esteem – for which they longed.

An accurate description of the harmful spiritual effects of the activities of the constructed personality is complicated at best. This description is especially complicated because a sort of mild social version of adapting to one's culture by adopting certain behaviors to go along with cultural requirements (like not murdering or abusing people who irritate us) is positive and essential to enculturation. But in this book I'm *not* talking about those virtually universal, benign, and even positive 'constructions.' I'm talking about a *deceptive* phenomenon that *sabotages* and *denies* the *basic integrity, direction, and soul* of the authentic person.

As previously suggested, there is a normal and healthy part of the child (and later the adult) that, although living through a constructed personality, does negotiate parts of life honestly and openly with others. But in cases where the shaming voices have been especially overbearing and the soul has been severely bound and imprisoned, the most important focus of the person's life energy is on the successful operation and defense of his or her carefully constructed (but false) personality and the goals of that personality. When the little soul is locked away and virtually incapacitated in 'the basement' of the almost sound-proof prison facade of the constructed personality, there is a strange inner sense of separation and lack of understanding of who one really is, and perhaps even a great deal of vocational restlessness.

Increasingly, then, we project to the world this new life invented (1) to please or at least win out over whoever the inner voices represent, and (2) to meet specific external criteria in the field of endeavor we have chosen. Unfortunately, when in this process, the constructed personality is not connected to our soul operationally, except in the most distant or tenuous way.

Interestingly, even though the overt behavioral characteristics of the constructed personality are not congruent with the values and integrity of the specific person's soul, the constructed personality is not necessarily that of an evil or 'dishonest' person. For example, as the story of Burt suggests, one might even unconsciously construct a personality designed to be a minister, an evangelist, a dedicated teacher, a physician, or a psychotherapist. He or she may study hard, pray, and know a great deal about medicine, religion, and God, yet for practical purposes the individual is not connected to his or her soul. Such a person may be very unhappy, even though extremely successful in his or her vocation! This type of respectable or successful construction makes it very difficult for such people to see that their lives are based on unreality and disconnected from their souls.

No matter what personality we choose to construct and develop, occasionally along the way we may hear, even from its jail, the faint echo of the little soul's 'Tweeeeet!!' calling to us as it keeps blowing the whistle on the unreality of our lives. We may only hear the verbal crying out of the soul occasionally, perhaps when we wake up at 4:00 A.M. from a bad dream and feel very uncomfortable about the way we are living.[6] Or we may be touched by our soul when we experience sadness about our 'unlived life and secret dreams' while watching a movie or reading a book. The soul embodies the positive deeper part of us that calls us to embrace and learn all we can that will lead us to *the truth that has our name on it*! The soul knows there is a part of us that is not really interested in our compliant people-pleasing personality or our constructed compulsive drive for success that pushes us forward to the point of exhaustion. Still, we rationalize that we *must not fail*, and we dismiss the soul's pleading voice as soon as possible, calling it 'neurotic, idealistic, or perfectionistic.' We charge on toward exaggerated success, or sink back toward being a self-effacing wimp to keep from being shamed, whichever kind of personality we have chosen to construct.

The cleverness of the human mind is absolutely amazing. The Bible talks about the deceptive and baffling way we good people can con ourselves into incredible unreality and wickedness: 'The heart is deceitful above all things, and desperately corrupt; who can understand it?' (Jer. 17:9).

8

A Look Behind the Curtain

BEFORE DESCRIBING THE INTENSE AND FRIGHTENING COURSE of the constructed personality's development, I want to pause and emphasize the ominous importance of this subtle disintegration of reality. To do that, I will present some candid 'snapshots' of the spiritual carnage of the constructed life that is seldom seen because it takes place behind the steely gossamer but opaque veil of denial.

The development of constructed personalities and the imprisonment of the reality-orienting soul is such a universal phenomenon that at first glance it may seem like the 'harmless way everyone grows up.' But this is not true. Although the constructed life may be normative, it is not spiritually healthy, in that it leads individuals and institutions very subtly and unconsciously into a kind of uncritical acceptance of dishonesty, misdirected lives, and even immorality – without their even seeing it happen.[1] An individual, a church, an educational or political system, or even a nation with a constructed personality can wind up living a dishonest and even immoral life – by its own standards – and not only be in denial about it but angrily project its denied dishonest, shadowy traits on other individuals, churches, political parties, or nations.[2]

When we detach from the soul and start hiding our true self from other people behind a constructed personality, we are locking in the closet our only accurate faculty that can reflect to us on a daily basis any dissonance between our behavior and our own true values. As a result of this separating isolation, our inner life can become a little like a 'house of mirrors' inside.

Have you ever been in a house of mirrors at an amusement park? You stand in front of one mirror and you appear to be slender and eight feet tall. Then step in front of another and you look broad-shouldered and strong – but very short and overweight. Whichever way you wish you were, you stand in front of *that* mirror and see yourself as you want to present yourself, and not as you really are.

That's something like what the constructed person's insides become – a distorted house of mirrors. After a while our skewed inner reality becomes who we are and what we perceive for all practical purposes. There is also much pressure to convince other people to agree to what we see ourselves and our lives to be. Thus, a strong parent with a rigid constructed personality can cause a whole family to silently agree to accept the parent's controlling style and picture of life as benevolent even though it is not true or rational for them. Parents may try to superimpose their constructed picture of life on themselves first, and then on their children, in some painful (but invisible to the world) ways.

1. DISHONESTY WITH SELF, OTHERS, AND GOD
When I began to construct a larger-than-life personality to quiet the shaming voices and get esteem out in the world, I

had to repress my vision of the person God made me to be. I had to build a whole life based on the unreality of other's shaming opinions, often distorted and delivered out of their anger or ignorance and based on their getting esteem from the world. This constructing process involved becoming or pretending to be whatever was necessary to get 'them' to like me, approve of me, or reward me. In other words, a life not based on *my* God-given aptitudes and dreams at all but on conforming to someone else's idea about who or what I should be is often based on *their* constructed needs.

For example, when I was a young boy I loved to read and to write stories; I dreamed of being a story-writer. I also loved my father and my older brother very much. But I was hurt constantly because my father obviously preferred to be with my older brother, Earle, who was a talented athlete. One day when I was about seven or eight, the three of us were sitting around the dinner table talking. My father said to me, 'Hey, Johnny, what do you want to be when you grow up?' He was a business man, an independent oil operator who searched for oil and gas fields. Being pleased to be addressed by him, I said (honestly and I'm sure with my face shining with excitement), 'I'd like to be a writer and write stories!'

My older brother laughed derisively, got up and began to dance around the room daintily, flapping his arms slowly and imitating a fairy while saying, 'Oh, isn't he *sweet*! He wants to be a *wri-i-i-ter*!' He acted as if anyone who wanted to be a writer was a 'fairy,' which in the male-dominated culture of Oklahoma at that time was *not* a flattering thing to say about a man. I looked at my father and he was smiling.

From that day on I became dishonest with myself and God and hid my true dreams of who I wanted to be. I not only never mentioned being a writer to my father again, but I decided writing *was* sissy and that I would become a businessman –

a better one than my father was. I forgot about wanting to be a writer and built a masculine, businessman constructed personality that included an intense interest in sports (which lasted beyond college athletics) and demanded that I get a degree in business administration – in which I made excellent grades, even though I was not very interested.

When I was in my twenties, and miserable starting out to be a high achiever for a major oil company, my father died. Within a few years I won a poetry contest and later wrote my first book – which sold all over the world. But my whole life until then had been lived (unconsciously) to get my father's esteem – and to avoid the shaming voices that said if I were to become a writer my sexual orientation might be in doubt to other people. As a result of getting back in touch with my soul and God, I got two other degrees – in theology and psychology/counseling – and have written or coauthored twenty-two books.

Over the years I have counseled many people who have skewed their entire vocational lives and ignored their aptitudes in order to construct an adequate personality designed to get esteem from someone else.

Although the kind of unconscious influencing by parents that I have described is very common and certainly not always that harmful, an awareness by parents that each child has special aptitudes that need to be discovered and nurtured – and that may be almost totally different from those of the parent or other children – can help children find and develop their own appropriate vocations and relationships more soundly and sanely.

2. MAKING THE WRONG PERSONAL
RELATIONSHIP CHOICES
Families' constructed personalities also affect the children's

choice of friends and mates profoundly. The way society is made up, some of this may be necessary, but I have counseled with many people who have been deeply hurt by the rigidity of a parent's constructed personality.

I'm thinking of an intelligent young nineteen-year-old woman. She met a man who seemed to be ideal for her soul. She fell in love with him, admired his integrity, his caring habits, his commitment to God. She had all kinds of common interests with him. He was intelligent and sensitive, and he adored her. After knowing him almost two years, she felt that he was really right for her. Everything she could get in touch with in her soul told her this was the right person for her to marry.

But because she was living in a family with a strong, unreal constructed personality, she didn't marry him – her mother didn't like the old car he drove. Although the daughter did not realize it, she was still trying to get love from her mother and father, so she denied the voice of her soul that had said, in its reaching out for perfect companionship, 'This is the one!' Instead, she married a young man from a wealthy family who was 'right' socially, even though he lacked the soul-mate compatibility of the other man. The chosen husband was apparently already an alcoholic in the learning stage, but because the family's constructed personality needed the social status more than the spiritual reality of the man, they manipulated the daughter into marrying the incompatible husband – to bring the family self-esteem and avoid a possible taint on their family constructed personality.

3. LIVING IN GRANDIOSITY THROUGH CONSTANT OVERCOMMITMENT

When one detaches from the soul and creates a larger-than-life personality, it is almost inevitable that the individual's perception will be skewed concerning what he or she can (or should) be able to be accomplish. I have talked to dozens of people who are exhausted by constant overcommitments, and who can't seem to get caught up or quit taking on too much. Without the reality-oriented soul to evaluate how much work or social activity is appropriate for a day, a week, or a month, the constructed personality with its inflated view of its abilities believes firmly, as part of its delusionary system, that it can, in fact, do the constantly overcommitted schedule *on time* – if other people wouldn't hold the person back or interrupt.

Harriet was a very intelligent wife and mother of three active children, ages three, five, and seven. She loved her husband, Roy, a rising star as an orthopedic surgeon. Their agreement had been that Harriet could follow her career as an attorney if she could manage it and still see to the care of the children. Harriet had built a constructed personality of a successful attorney who was also a super wife and super mom. She had been told by her conservative parents that it was shameful not to take care of your family and that no woman could be a successful attorney like Harriet's father was and raise a family too.

But Harriet was totally organized. She had yearly, monthly, and weekly goals for every area of her life, and for a while, to everyone's amazement, she was able to carry it off. Her friends (with some jealousy) called her 'Wonder Girl.'

Then everything ballooned. Roy became very well known, and professional athletic teams from all over the country sent patients to him. As the three boys got older, two were outstanding athletes and one was a club joiner and drama king. And at the same time, Harriet's law practice experienced a growth spurt.

Harriet quit getting enough sleep, working far into the nights on her legal work so she could take time to watch her children perform – often reading from her briefcase in the bleachers. She started being late everywhere – something she had never done. She also began having a couple of drinks to calm her nerves in the evenings. People at her office told her she was trying to do too much. She and Roy began to see each other less and less, and when they were together, they argued – often about the fact that Harriet had 'dried up and blown away emotionally' from the family. Still, throughout it all, Harriet maintained that she could handle everything; she just needed a little space from the family to get things caught up. But she never did. After three years of trying to get Harriet to go get help, Roy left. She felt betrayed and blamed him for not being understanding.

Harriet might never have seen the bizarre grandiosity of her constructed personality if she hadn't become an alcoholic, had a wreck, and been sent to treatment.

4. CONSTRUCTED SOCIAL RELATIONSHIPS
AND POSSESSIONS

Because the constructed person has myopic vision focused on his or her own goals, almost all the person's relationships are (bottom line) strongly pragmatic and self-centered – even if the constructed personality is that of an unselfish Christian or even a minister. The constructed person consciously or semi-consciously measures people and social interactions on the basis of how much they might further his or her plans and deliver esteem and love to the secret inner 'counting-house' of the person's life. This leads to a web of small insignificant social habits that are not exactly God's way of operating.

For example, when I was a young businessman attending a party or other gathering of people, if I met someone who might further my constructed course, I'd spend a good bit of the evening talking with him or her. On meeting other people who weren't useful to what I needed for my constructed personality, I would say, 'Hi, it's very good to meet you,' and move on. This may seem like a little innocent thing, but when we are not living out the authentic loving behaviors we are preaching about and presenting ourselves as engaged in, the cumulative effect is unreal and the opposite of love and integrity.

Our constructed person often chooses possessions and friends who will complete the cast and stage set of that constructed personality's carefully edited dream: perhaps friends who look good, smell good, and have big cars. People with grandiose constructed personalities spend money they don't have to buy cars that will make them feel adequate – even when the car they traded in ran like a top. Others choose friends who are 'intellectuals,' or earthy nonconformist friends who take pride in wearing old clothes and driving old cars.

When I started this book we owned two old cars, and in the church we go to that sometimes made me uneasy. Still, I don't have any debt at all, I'm happy, and I'm able to do the things I want to do. Things were different twenty years ago. Because of my constructed personality, I used to drive Mercedes cars. Now, a Mercedes is an excellent car for many people and will last forever – at least that's how I rationalized my purchase. But the truth is my constructed personality was supposed to be financially successful. I wanted people to know I was doing well, wanted it enough to buy very expensive cars.

For a long time when I was in the oil exploration business I couldn't figure out why I didn't enjoy going to parties. I remember how strange it seemed *not* to want to go to a lovely party with beautiful people. I enjoyed the people when I had relationships of the soul with them, but usually none of those people were there, and I'd get bored to death. I was bored because I was not there for a 'real reason.' I was there because my constructed personality said I was *supposed* to be there. I didn't have any energy for parties, so I drank, which seemed to give me a little energy. I learned that drinking allowed me to do things I didn't really want to do, to be with people I didn't want to be with. I went to those parties because my constructed personality's agenda was evidently more important than living a sane life with more time to read and rest, and with less pretentious but more compatible friends.

The point is that our constructed personalities can push us to get unreal friends, unreal lovers, unreal spouses, unreal jobs, unreal clothes, unreal cars, and even unreal houses to satisfy the insatiable craving of the constructed personality for things designed to bring us self-esteem and quiet the shaming voices that say we are not good enough.

5. CONSTRUCTED CHOICE OF RELIGIOUS AFFILIATION

The insidiousness of the constructed personality's approach to life is that many times we cannot see the obvious self-defeating aspects of our choices. For instance, when we live beyond our incomes continually to 'be enough,' we become financially stressed and eventually may *lose* esteem. But because the constructed personality is separated from its reality checker, it can easily be blinded by its materialism, or elitism, or any one of a number of philosophies and even theologies that do not bring the spiritual fulfillment the constructed personality longs for so desperately.

For example, although this was a real shock when I discovered it, when I chose a Christian denomination to be a part of, it was largely on the basis of the image my constructed personality needed. I definitely did not want to be in certain denominations because the people in them didn't fit my constructed image. I never looked at their theologies seriously. I found bad points about their thinking or behavior so I could rationalize not being one of them, and even made fun of some of them subtly to distance myself from them. I'm almost weeping as I write this, but I was not aware of how what I was doing revealed the shallowness of my constructed personality and the separation it caused me from some delightful and intelligent Christians. Over the years I have discovered that my soul sometimes has more in common with other social groups, economic groups, and religious denominations than the ones I chose while entrenched in the building of my constructed personality.

The hope of avoiding the shaming voices and being adequate can make us live the way I've described in this chapter. Even appearing to be adequate will do for some. Our friend, Howard Butt, Jr, and his wife, Barbara Dan, went to New York years ago. They went to see the Broadway musical *South Pacific*, which was sold out. After the show Howard saw scalpers selling ticket *stubs* with a program. People who hadn't been able to get in bought these stubs and programs and evidently took them back home to Texas, California, or wherever, put the ticket stubs and the program on their coffee table, and hummed a few bars of 'Some Enchanted Evening' to give the impression they had actually been to see the show. This is a humorous yet sad example, but it illustrates the lengths to which some people may go in their constructed lives. Still, it's not that different from the way many of us live in our constructed personalities. When we do things we don't want to do and buy things we don't really care about to bolster our faltering self-esteem, we may never experience the real drama – the love, the peace, and the sense of well being.

In a constructed personality we often buy the program and the ticket stubs of life, but do we ever see the show?

Part 2

En Route to the Pinnacle

Introduction to Part 2

WHEN A CHILD IS GROWING UP AND UNCONSCIOUSLY PUTTING together a constructed personality, he or she experiments with various behaviors, almost like trying on clothes to see what fits. And the early stages of building can be exciting and sometimes painful.

For example, in order to be 'a man,' I imitated my older brother and father by being profane. I swore like a sailor. My mother was not pleased at all, but since I wanted esteem from my father and brother more than I wanted to comply with her language code, I kept taking on behavior and habits evidently designed to make me appear to be a virile Southerner/ Southwesterner. This also meant having a great interest in sports, so I went for sports. In addition, my mother had drummed into me the fact that virile men who weren't smart and sensitive were not respected by grown-up men and women. Therefore I added to my construction a secret plan to do well in school and be sensitive. And although I was shy and afraid of getting close to girls, I pushed myself through my fear to talk to them, listen to them, and speak to them by name when most boys ignored them.

The secret price I paid to become this constructed paragon of manhood was, I now see, almost unbelievable. For example, by the time I got to high school I wanted to make the basketball team. The only problem was that although I had played basketball in gym classes in junior high, I'd never even seen a high school basketball game until the ninth grade, and the high school I went to was very large and competitive. I soon found out what I needed to do to succeed as a basketball player and paid the price to get in excellent condition. I was only 5' 7" when I tried out, so I knew I would have to learn to jump higher than the other players.

At night I went out in our family's garage, climbed a ladder against the wall, and drove a nail in six inches higher than I had ever been able to jump. Then I kept jumping, over and over again, night after night, until I touched the nail. Then I raised it six inches. I ran, did pushups, and stayed after practice day after day after day, shooting each shot I wanted to master dozens and dozens and dozens of times.

I grew five inches the summer before my junior year and made both the team and all-conference the same season. I learned virtually everyone's name at school and applied myself in all areas.

By the time I finished college my constructed package seemed complete enough to allow me to become very successful and to win the esteem I felt would only come with great achievement.

I was afraid, but excited. I had no idea why I was so insecure inside or why I rationalized so much and had trouble making decisions. Without realizing what I was doing, I had built a very dedicated high-flying constructed personality – and locked my reality-checking soul in the prison of my unconscious. I was ready to begin the run for success in America!

9

Cracks in the Foundation

AT FIRST GLANCE THE SOUL'S SPIRITUAL ADVENTURE APPEARS to end with its imprisonment and the formation of a constructed personality. It often seems like the compulsive constructed life can't fail to flourish and win big time, sealing the soul forever in an impregnable prison. But when we live our lives out of touch with reality, sooner or later a subtle spiritual disintegration process begins that quietly and patiently eats at the foundation of all that is unreal. No matter how successful the inauthentic personality may become in the world, eventually, as in bad cement, cracks appear in the foundation and walls of the tallest towers, or the most successful personalities, that can be constructed.

This disintegration process will be different for each person according to the type of constructed personality they have developed. If the aim is to build a powerful and successful life – a strong image – in order to quiet the shame voices and get self-esteem, then the constructing and disintegration process may be more public. Whereas if one is trying to construct an image of a humble servant, a dedicated mom, a long-suffering spouse of an alcoholic, or compulsive achiever – lives of apparent sacrifice and weakness – the struggles to avoid failure may be more secretive and undetectable, at least until the last stages.

What evidently happens in virtually all cases, though, is that we wind up in a desperate losing struggle to *save* the very things we construct these unreal personalities to get:

1) intimacy, love, and the connectedness that will overcome our basic loneliness and
2) the success and self-esteem for which we long to quiet the shaming voices.

The Destruction of Intimacy with Others

Authentic intimacy between persons – that sharing of personal reality without either party being fixed or manipulated – is one of the most joyful and nourishing experiences of the soul, even if the content of the reality shared is sometimes painful.

Authentic intimacy creates an atmosphere in which two souls can share happiness, pain, fear, and imperfection but also where they can relax and 'come out and play.' One such experience is that of falling in love. Sometimes when two people fall in love, they put a hold on the pretensions of their constructed personalities, open the door to their playful honest souls, and let their beloved see them, warts and all. The initial fear is that the other will run away – but when that doesn't happen, both parties may say, 'Hurrah, I'm home free. No judgment here!' Then they may marry their beloved. But too often the door of intimacy either does not open in courtship, or it closes after the wedding (or the honeymoon) and one or both of the parties goes back into their controlling constructed personalities.

The problem seems to be that we learn to hide and protect our skewed version of our reality as we construct our personalities to (1) quiet the shaming voices inside that say we aren't enough (important and rich enough if we go for 'strong,' or humble and saintly enough if we opt for a 'weak' strategy), and (2) to get esteem from others out in the world. Besides our marital choice, other parts of our (secretly) self-centered construction package will strongly influence the way we choose and maintain our intimate relationships, the sort of home we live in, and how we relate all this to our 'primary esteem acquiring vehicle' (i.e., vocation, intimate relationship, outstanding children, etc.).

By the time the builder of a constructed personality gets through adolescence, he or she has usually made a fair beginning on the construction of a personality with which to successfully navigate the storms of early adulthood.

I had evidently decided that I had to be important; win big; be an athlete; be a sensitive, sexy male; and be smart. This made for a very busy life in high school and college. In my senior year at the university I married a yearbook beauty. It all looked great.

But the problems with intimacy came when I got married. Inside the silver armor of this successful white knight image of a college man was a frightened little boy who felt shamefully inadequate. My shaming voices had pointed out that I was a fraud because in basketball I had made all-conference but not all-state in high school, because I had not made the first team at the university before I broke my neck as a sophomore (on a team that was second in the nation the year before), and because I felt like I was unattractive and not really smart – I 'just barely' made the Business Administration

School's honorary scholastic society, Gamma Phi Beta.

Yet when I married a very attractive honor student, I had put the crown on my constructed personality's agenda. I had married a queen. The problem was that the difference between my constructed personality's achievement record and my inner lack of self-esteem was incredible.

Since intimacy is the sharing of our true feelings, as well as our thoughts, I was in trouble. We could talk about our future, but because my reality-checking soul was securely locked in prison, I had no idea about what I wanted to be after college. I just knew I *had* to succeed. In hopes of winning my father's love, I had taken his advice and gotten a degree in finance. By the time of graduation, however, I realized I didn't even like business or finance. Still my constructed personality was programmed to succeed, so off we went into the oil exploration business.

In my marriage, true intimacy was hard for me to come by. Because I was out of touch with who I really was underneath my achievements, I couldn't share my personal reality and what my dreams for the future were – I wasn't in touch with that part of me. Although it worried me when I thought about it, I still 'didn't know what I wanted to be when I grew up.' Still I kept working at laying new foundations for success, and success began to come. But authentic intimacy shriveled somehow.

Intimacy didn't get easier because so much of the success I did get seemed unreal or undeserved to me. Therefore self-defeating constructed habits to hide my inadequacy began to emerge. For example, when I would get very insecure, I would start bragging about what was going on in my work life, to what grand place I'd been, with what important person I'd had lunch, and so forth. I almost weep when I think about doing this because I hate this in myself, this self-centered grandiosity that is supposed to mask my insecurity. But I know now that when I am sharing as a way to make myself appear to be more adequate than I feel, the sharing has a hollow ring and ultimately has the opposite effect from the one I intend. Such bragging can be very destructive to an intimate relationship when the one bragging is not able to share his or her real feelings (fears, adequacies), or admit being wrong, and hides such feelings instead by presenting a false but adequate-looking self.

Actually, the constructed personality is better at emotional 'one-night stands.' I'm not talking about sexual encounters, but a one-night stand in the sense of being able to share reality for an evening. We may be good at having short relationships, or relationships designed so we only have to spend time occasionally with the other person; then we can keep up the protective constructed walls. That's one of the reasons I think Freud believed the psychotherapy sessions ought to be almost every day. It is much more difficult to hold one's defensive constructed self together and stay in control of the relationship after a number of intense consecutive periods of sharing.

Over the years I have seen how constructed personalities can cripple or destroy intimate relationships for other reasons besides one or both parties being increasingly out of touch with their reality, their souls. For example, our unconscious (constructed) expectations about how our intimate relationships should be lived out – including everything from attitudes toward sexual relations to what kind of car or house a couple should have – can be invisible minefields for constructed personalities in their search for intimacy. The following story illustrates my point.

Dot and Jack got married, and after their honeymoon began dreaming about having a family and building a house. What neither realized was that their unconscious expectations were based on their separate personal constructed personalities, which were very different from each other's. Dot began dreaming and talking about a home and a family that was based unconsciously on the rules and expectations of the family in which she was raised – the same family from which she got the shame and fearful prohibitions that helped form her constructed personality. She was from a wealthy family but had felt ashamed of their affluence, and the ostentatious home her parents had built, and their large black Cadillac. Also a wealthy neighbor child was kidnapped when Dot was six.

As a consequence of these and many other things, Dot's expectations had been formed. She wanted a small, but very nice house in an exclusive, guarded neighborhood, and a small white car. She told Jack she would feel safer with a high wall around the property and only elevated or narrow windows in the outside walls of the house. She wanted the children to play in their own yard 'where they'll be safe.'

Meanwhile at the same address, Jack was thinking about a very different scenario. Having been raised in a poor family, Jack wanted a large home as part of his intention to be successful and wealthy. He was dreaming about building a home based on another set of rules and expectations that he learned as a child and that helped form his constructed personality. Jack craved the freedom and breathing room afforded by a spacious open lot with no walls around it and lots of large windows in the house to let in the light and fresh air. He wanted a lot of expensive 'rolling stock.' He also wanted his children to be free to play with other children in the neighbors' yard or invite the neighbors' kids to play in their yard when they wanted to.

Because the two families in which the couple were raised were not alike, their resulting constructed lives had very different agendas. The couple warred over whose constructed personality was going to prevail concerning the rules and ways of living in their new life together. Although they both knew that some disagreements were normal, both Jack and Dot were amazed and appalled at how *entrenched* the other was in having his or her own way. With those different attitudes, the home and family life designed by the couple had very little of the intimacy between souls that had prevailed in their courting days. Instead, they began constantly to bicker about the material expressions of their inherited rules of living, neither of which were totally appropriate in some ways to their young family's financial situation.

The point here is that when one person's constructed personality gets threatened for *whatever* reason by the other, the threatened party can experience baffling but intense fear – and anger. Intimacy is often the first thing to go, as one or both get the bit in their teeth and charge on to the building of their constructed personality's dreams – because these very personal expectations *feel* like they are *obviously* the *right way* to do things.

'Intimacy' as a Part of a Constructed Personality

Almost everybody is frightened of intimacy at some level, but I have a confession to make: I haven't appeared to be as scared as most because intimacy has been a part of my constructed package. I was trained by my mother to 'do' intimacy, and I longed for it. I 'out-intimacied' almost everybody I knew. But when intimacy becomes a component of a constructed personality, *a mechanism* to bring us esteem and love, we can become emotionally a kind of seductive pain bringer as we seem to be promising something we actually *can't* deliver. We can't be truly intimate over a long period because the only thing we can talk about is our constructed reality with its consciously or unconsciously edited thoughts, feelings, and dreams.

I learned to talk *about* spiritual things, *about* personal reality, but I almost always stayed on ground that was safe for me, and was often not really vulnerable. I *looked* intimate, and I felt as intimate as I thought I was, only somehow, sometimes, there was not a connection for me between what I said and the deepest part of me. There was something about my sharing that made me nervous (it also made other people nervous I've discovered, years after the fact). Having to have constant surveillance and unconsciously editing for adequacy made me feel alone and isolated much of the time, even though intimacy was my style and I was consciously sincere.

There are many reasons why intimacy disintegrates as people move from courtship into marriage or from acquaintanceship into the deeper stages of friendship. Intimacy between children, parents, and other family members is often injured or destroyed as children construct, or parents defend, their unreal constructed personalities.[1] The sad thing is that the constructed personality's purpose in going for success and approval is to get self-esteem that is supposed to bring intimacy and love with others, God, and oneself. But all these possibilities for intimacy are either incapacitated or destroyed when they get in the path of the driving constructed personality with its self-centered goals and expectations, which feel like they were written in stone and passed down the mountain from Moses to us by God Himself.

If the conflicting expectations cannot be negotiated, one or both parties in a relationship may stay in the relationship but desert the other emotionally and bury himself or herself in fulfilling the vocational or personal goals of his or her own constructed personality. Efforts to achieve intimacy may virtually disappear. I believe this situation is much more common than many people might think – even in families where the partners are physicians, psychotherapists, teachers, or ministers.

But, if one party threatens to leave the relationship, and having that relationship is an integral part of the *other* party's constructed life's picture, a powerful and devastating replacement for intimacy may enter and dominate the couple's life: control.

Control: The Dark Underside of Intimacy

When the longing for intimacy in a relationship has been blocked or denied by the self-defeating behavior of constructed personalities, there often arises an urgent need in one or both partners to get control of the other party. In fact, under the threat of losing a close relationship, the constructed personality sometimes forgets about its goals in the future and redoubles its efforts to control everything and everyone important to him or her in the present.

I certainly did that. And my spiritual counseling with other Christians who have come to me for help indicates that a lot of good Christians with constructed personalities do that. We become very controlling, yelling (or hissing) at our families and openly advising or 'hinting' blame and advice about how they should live their lives. As we start intensifying these control behaviors, this increased controlling starts a terrible self-defeating downward spiral in the life and relationships of the controller. As others accuse us of trying to run their lives, and reject that which our constructed personality tells us is 'helping' them, we get more defensive, angry, and frantic to give them advice or fix them. But often they just get more and more ready to run away.

Part of the reason we need to be a fixer (when living in a

crumbling constructed personality) is that we're living in an increasingly unreal and irrational constructed world. It becomes more and more difficult to validate that world by getting others to accept it and the terms of its goals as these relate to them (like staying married). Because of our Sin, our bent to put ourselves in the center and be number one, we feel that we have to validate our perceptions and justify ourselves.

Sometimes people with shaky constructed personalities seek unwise intimacy with men or women outside their marriage who will verify the attractiveness of their constructed personality. In such cases very sharp disagreements can arise at home, often escalating into separations, divorces, or children telling controlling parents they aren't going to relate to them at all any more, and running away. Many families scratch their heads in anger and frustration, wondering how they got into these apparently irreconcilable wars and isolated camps.

We cannot share intimately for fear of revealing our unacceptable (and unreal) manipulative constructed personality. When people close to us begin to see and point out the inconsistencies between our outwardly honest and sensitive constructed selves and our inward dishonesty and lack of sensitive sharing, a crisis may begin to brew on the horizon. When we begin to try to control people's reality (i.e., their perception about who we are, who they are, and how we should live together) and try to 'fix them' and run their lives, sooner or later they are very likely to back off emotionally – and sometimes physically – leaving us in a whole different kind of loneliness than many of us have experienced before.

The pain of this lonely sense of isolation often drives the constructed self to redouble its efforts to meet its goals to get esteem through hard work. But because of the unconscious bent in human nature to be number one at any cost, and because we are increasingly out of touch with reality, this redoubling of our efforts to succeed and get esteem leads to new kinds of conflict and self-sabotage that can destroy the very dream of self-esteem that started the constructed adventure in the first place. When intimacy has failed, the longing for esteem may be the only hope the constructed self has left.

10

The Destruction of Self-Esteem

THE BASIC PROBLEM WITH CONSTRUCTING A PRESENTING personality to better negotiate life and win self-esteem is that the construction is not basically real, does not have structural integrity. For example, in the building business, if you have too much sand in the concrete that you pour into the foundation, you are setting yourself up for almost certain disaster. And the bigger the construction project and the faster it is built, the more likely a weak foundation will crack and begin to disintegrate early on. Because the purpose of the personality being constructed is to assure approval and self-esteem, any cracks showing up in the foundation can lead to intense concern and fears of failure. Here's how that seems to work when intimacy seems to fade or fail, and one focuses almost totally on achieving the constructed personality's goals.

The First Crack: A 'Small' Lack of Integrity

With the soul locked in prison, we can create an honest-looking, productive, successful, and very ethical or even religious outer life that other people see. At the same time we may develop another invisible side of our constructed personality that is calculating and controlling, and about which we are often in denial. This inner side to our outer exaggerated self is where we can cover our tracks; plan manipulations to control others and our environments in order to maintain the appearance of adequacy, integrity, and congruence; and harbor our vain, resentful, grandiose, and immoral thoughts. We may be more or less conscious of this duality but often brush it off as 'just being the way life is.'

If our young constructed personalities develop and succeed in the world – and things seem to be working for us – we can plan and later justify cutting corners with regard to rigorous honesty in our vocational lives and personal relationships. We can even be in denial about our motivations for 'doing good things,' and in our constructed personality's amazing self-justifying war room we can also rationalize resenting people and fueling hatreds, jealousies, and covetousness – some may even plan and later commit adultery, theft, or murder – justifying or denying our true motives the whole time. We can do all these things in our constructed inner life because (1) we have the ability to keep a secret, and (2) we have imprisoned our soul – the conscience part of our imperfect selves designed to evaluate as well as insist on the reality and integrity of our thoughts and actions. The stage is set for a myriad of subtly dishonest but denied behaviors.

This is one of the situations in which the invisible influence of Sin, our bent to be number one and replace God, can really get active. We can put aside the ethical rules we were taught as children as we feel lured toward situations and behaviors that might make us feel momentary esteem but will wind up separating us from people and principles we believe in – even from God.

Specific Dishonest and 'Slick' Behaviors Develop

This unconscious dishonesty often begins to develop through 'little' things that we do to keep from risking being rejected. The dishonest habits can begin with what seem to be mild, innocuous social patterns, but can slide imperceptibly into very serious chameleon-like personality vacillations and later into large immoral or unethical decisions.

A woman recently told me that the leaders in her Episcopal church decided that the people could choose to stand rather than kneel while receiving communion. Although it was clearly stated that either standing or kneeling was acceptable, she felt much more comfortable kneeling. However, she told me that she had begun to stand, because almost everyone in authority (whose approval her constructed personality desperately needed) had decided to stand at that time in the service. Although kneeling before God when receiving communion had a very high value for her, it was obviously not as high as her need for approval and esteem from the leading people in her church – whom she barely knew.

Given the opportunity, this same lack of integrity can be expanded to a larger state, involve many other people, and have great financial and legal consequences. For example, in 1996 there was an article in the *Wall Street Journal* about a group of outstanding Christian businessmen in America who were being accused of conning foundations and other wealthy Christians out of several hundreds of millions of dollars. Knowing about some of their lives and work, I would have thought that the men who apparently perpetrated this scam had integrity. But if the allegations are true, somehow in midlife these men evidently stepped out and 'forgot' or rationalized their Christian ethics, sabotaged themselves, hurt other people and their work, and ruined their own lives – at least the lives of their Christian constructed personalities.

As the habits of rationalizing and self-justifying increase, the constructed self may invent a working morality that shields the deep separation between our true but buried values and our behavior. In my case, I first became conscious of my constructed personality's lack of congruence when I saw that I was hiding my honest feelings because of the fear of exposure as not being intelligent and 'up' on what was going on that intelligent folk should know. This fear caused me to develop some dishonest habits and, in some areas, a vacillating personality, although I wasn't aware that I was doing anything wrong. For example, at a social gathering someone important might ask, 'What do you believe about the way the government is handling immigration?' I might ask in return, 'What do *you* think about that?' That way I could hear what the important person believed and then instantly (but *unconsciously* at the time I was doing so) edit my true feelings when I replied so as to appear to agree with the person to whom I was talking (more than I did) and not be rejected by that person – and still trying to express an honest opinion. Of course, that behavior was not honest, but rather was a sort of cosmetic surgery on the truth.

Spiritual Cosmetic Implant: A False Soul, A False Morality

As the constructed personality becomes more successful, the false implant process can become more complex, burying the soul even deeper in the integrity prison where we've incarcerated it. We may even begin to believe fervently the false morality we espouse is real. We start to rationalize instantly everything from spending money on luxuries we don't need or can't afford by convincing ourselves that we need them, to cheating on income taxes, expenses, or spouses 'because that's the way everybody lives now.' All such behaviors and rationalizations increase our denial about the fact that we have imprisoned our souls. Before long, we may *be convinced* that we have a fully developed and high morality based on the soul's highest values. Great moral leaders agree, however, that the bottom-line test of our morality is always reflected by the way we *act*, not what we profess (see Matt. 12:33–37).

Whatever one may think or say about honesty, the constructed personality's *operational* morality is determined by whatever will enhance or maintain the reputation and appearance of the constructed personality or overcome its pain and fear. But because of denial we cannot usually *see* our dishonesty with ourselves except in crisis situations.

The Painful Blow: Discovering Dishonesty with One's Self

One of the biggest blows to self-esteem on the secret adventure of our constructed life concerns the *discovery of one's denial* about an important tenet of a constructed life. Often our first conscious major clue that we are not spiritually healthy comes when we must face the fact that we have deluded ourselves and been dishonest concerning who we really are – and even about what we truly believe. In fact we may discover that what we *truly* believe (in our soul) directly contradicts or threatens our presenting constructed personality's beliefs. Josh was my first encounter with a man who in a crisis discovered that he wasn't at all the man he had always presented himself to be, and honestly thought he was.

Josh, a powerfully built man about forty years old, came to see me. He was confused and agitated when he sat down. Josh was a devout member of a religious group that has always been known for its strong witness in favor of peace and nonviolence. He worked in the security department on the campus of a large state university in the South and was very popular with the students. At various times when he was off duty, Josh had bull sessions with some of them.

One day, a few days before he came to my office, Josh had gotten into a heated argument about the spiritual value of a peace witness. The two young men he was talking to were football players who were definitely 'hawks' when it came to settling international disputes. After about an hour of trying to convince these young men that God wants Christians to settle all differences only with a peace witness, some inflammatory words were exchanged. Finally Josh got irritated and then angry. Losing all patience, he grabbed the larger boy by his shirt front and busted him on the mouth with his fist. In the fight that ensued, Josh did a pretty good job of beating up both young men. As a result he was fired from his job and censured by his church.

Among other things, I realized after some conversation that Josh was very *sincere* in his beliefs: he was dedicated to putting God first and sincerely believed in nonviolence as the way to resolve conflict. But as it turned out, these beliefs were a part of a fairly rigid religious constructed personality. When he was tested in a real, personal conflict, his constructed personality's faith failed, revealing his own deep but *unconscious* and dormant primary commitment to violence as the way to respond to perceived attack. This encounter revealed the unreal nature – a crack in the foundation – of his constructed personality that had been designed unconsciously to get love and esteem from his fellow believers.

Josh's story highlights the fact that when the soul is not allowed to be on duty to evaluate and insist on reality and integrity, the constructed personality is likely to be a potential loose cannon morally, and the 'host' person may be *amazed* when she or he is caught in a very dishonest, immoral, or inconsistent act. Examples of people to whom immorality 'just happened' after years in public and sincere helping professions are legion these days (e.g., the respectable psychiatrists, physicians, 'honest' politicians, and ministers of large and small churches and television ministries who have been caught doing immoral things).

When the constructed personality is in enough conflict and pain, or threatened with rejection, that personality may either throw over its belief openly, as Josh did, or rationalize and secretly seek an easier, softer way – a remedy that feels good to alleviate the pain, but often a remedy that neither the soul nor the constructed personality's public image would ever approve. As an example, after a serious marital argument or immoral betrayal (such as discovering that one's spouse has been unfaithful), the righteously offended constructed personality of the betrayed person may rationalize committing his or her own equally immoral act, like committing adultery, as being his or her legitimate 'due.'

Any person with a constructed personality may eventually reveal his lack of integrity and congruence by his actions under pressure. The revelation of these cracks in the structure of the constructed personality are very shaming and damaging to the already shaky self-esteem beneath the inflated construction.

Usually, sooner or later, other people who are important to us may begin to see the cracks in our constructed foundation and realize that we are not what we are presenting ourselves to be. In fact, this awareness can be a normal part of maturing, to recognize that all people have some areas of inconsistency and to become willing to accept them with some faults. But when people close to those of us with compulsive constructed personalities try to point out our inconsistencies, we may respond with strong denial to their observations. We may fight to rationalize our mistakes or blame them on circumstances or those close to us. When threatened with failure or exposure, we may feel an intensification of the anxiety and fear most people with longstanding constructed lives live with constantly.

As the cracks in the constructed personality become unmistakable, the trembling, fearful constructed life gets more painful and frantic inside. In time the fruitless redoubling of our efforts to succeed seem hollow, frenetic, and ineffective. When what we are doing is not connected with who we are in our souls, redoubling our efforts can become the beginning of a subtle sort of spiritual suicide. We may even begin to lose touch with objective reality and make serious and irrational vocational or personal decisions because our thinking is seriously clouded by panic and pain.

The resistance in my life to being able to see and own my problems and character defects was deeply entrenched. I made bad decisions and took incredibly stupid risks during my high dives on the 'bungee-jumps' my constructed personality kept insisting that I take – sometimes without being properly attached – so I wouldn't have to face the deep fear of failure and being considered the inept coward my shaming voices had told me I was.

For example, during this frightening period in my life, I got angry at a business associate because he made what I considered a mistake and wouldn't do what I wanted to correct it. Instead of calmly trying to work through the problem, in my pride and anger I did an insane thing: broke the relationship and sold some securities he was managing for me, taking an unnecessary twenty-thousand-dollar loss I couldn't afford – and could have avoided. I made an inexcusably bad business decision because I was angry at the man and felt that he didn't respect me. I *had* to be *right*! As a person who majored in finance, I realized I had made a very irrational move. But the fears and lack of esteem I was feeling concerning the other areas of my life and relationships blotted out the seriousness of what I had done. Making irrational, self-defeating mistakes to try to shore up faltering self-esteem is common when one's constructed personality is beginning to crack at the foundational level.

When such mistakes come to light, the shaming voices come roaring out like clawing hungry lions to terrorize the constructed self and fight over the carcass of any self-esteem that may be left.

The Lost Soul Complex

The constructed personality may have become more and more proficient in the building stages, but as that happens we may become less and less in touch in any dynamic way with our reality-checking, whistle-blowing soul. As the spiritual disintegration process begins and continues, we are less and less conscious of who we really are and what we really want in life.

After a while we may be separated from people, God, and our good intentions. We may be in denial and we may not even be aware that the spiritually ungrounded personality we have constructed can hurt, abuse, or desert other people close to us in its headlong dash for success and esteem. In fact, as these things happen, we often believe that we are very honest, spiritual, and loving spouses, parents, children, and friends. And we may be baffled that people don't seem to approve of us or like us.

An example is Mark, a thirty-year-old home-builder who was a busy, independent contractor. When Mark met Cindy, a cute, intelligent, live wire type of person, he soon was in love in a way he never had been. And an amazing thing happened that often takes place when people fall in love. Mark's strong serious 'successful-building-contractor-personality' was put aside, and somehow he let his carefree childlike soul come out on parole to play with Cindy. That's who Cindy fell in love with.

Several years later, when Mark came to me, he was very disturbed because Cindy, now his wife, had told him that he was an 'absentee father' to his six- and four-year-old sons. 'And you're giving me zip!' she'd said. 'Where did the guy on the white horse go who swept me up in his arms and carried me across the threshold?'

Mark continued to tell his story, 'Last night Cindy said to me, "Mark, for the past eight months you've turned out all your 'sexual and intimate conversation lights' when you turned off the truck ignition in the garage. I'm tired of living with a play-like spouse. I don't know what's happened, but there's something really screwy. You can either get some help, or the kids and I are out of here . . . or rather, *you're* out of here!"'

Mark was obviously floored by what Cindy had said. In a

distant way he realized that Cindy had been trying to talk to him, but it was always 'at the wrong time.' He sighed. 'I was so busy providing for my family that I was too tired to deal with their problems when I got home.' Mark saw himself as a dedicated contractor, committed family man, active churchman, and a rising young star in the Rotary Club. He even got the kids up and played with them many Saturday mornings. What more could a wife want? He thought he was doing everything right. People all over town thought he was a good churchman and family man.

Although Mark said he was 'home four or five evenings a week,' Cindy had said that he always came in just in time for supper and brought a briefcase full of paperwork with which he disappeared after the meal. By the time eleven o'clock came around (Mark later admitted in counseling), he was too tired to make love or even talk to Cindy about it. But he said that he *did* talk to her at bedtime – a lot – even though he was exhausted. Cindy, however, had said Mark didn't talk about anything personal when he was getting ready for bed. Instead, he gave long monologue reports on what he was doing at work or replayed conversations with important clients he'd seen.

Mark had built a classic 'successful-business-and-community-family-man' constructed personality. As his financial success had grown, Mark had become increasingly separated from his childlike soul, with whom Cindy had fallen in love. He had left Cindy and his children in an emotional desert – even though, as he said defensively, 'I spend more time at home with my family than any man I know!' Yet his family felt like they were a cross between his emotional furniture and unappreciated bit players in his life's drama. Mark could not see that he was at fault in Cindy's problem. He maintained that he was a good father and husband and that all the work he was doing was for 'for *them*.'

Mark loved his family, but he thought he was right and was doing a good job as a husband and father. He might have left at that point, but his constructed life did not include divorce. This predicament led him into a lot of pain before he finally went for help and began the trip toward a healed marriage and the freeing of his imprisoned soul.

How Can We Get Help?

If we are fortunate, things finally start falling apart enough that we *recognize* we are stuck somehow and start seeing signs that our constructed efforts are really floundering. People important to us, who care for us, may try to reach out to us – as Cindy did to Mark – and tell us how we are in trouble and that our behavior is hurting them. When that happens, our fear of being exposed as inadequate by their view of us raises the interior voice of our fear a hundred decibels; we become afraid that they might desert us or we might drive them away.

At this point we may look for help to stop the exodus.

11

Going for Help: Powerlessness

AFTER MUCH STRUGGLE MANY PEOPLE GET EXHAUSTED, OVER-committed, and out of control trying to be or look like they are more or better than they really are, as they defend and justify their incongruent behavior. Yet because of the need to look adequate, nobody else may know that within them the tension of the warfare has been increasing exponentially. No one sees that their inner awareness is constricting inside an ever tightening circle of bad relationships, of dread – a vortex of anxiety winding a choking rope of fear around the neck of the constructed personality.

Finally, in bewilderment and intense frustration at not being able to fix things and reverse the downward trajectory of their constructed lives, people make a big change. Suddenly they start wanting to simply *get rid of their pain and fear and feel better*, whatever the cost. They secretly try to find something to do or someone to go to who soothes or medicates the untenable pain and fear brought on by their lonely control attempts and the rejection they cause. Some of these attempts at medication are: drinking too much, eating too much, over-working, being falsely nice and accommodating, compulsively increasing religious activities, sexual acting out, or any one of dozens of other compulsive or addictive behaviors.

We overdo any of these unwise or sinful activities because we are in pain and can't face our reality (though we may justify our actions as being because 'we deserve some R and R'). Thus we try to rationalize or minimize our self-defeating behavior to make our constructed personality feel, 'I really am okay, you see,' or 'I do all this work at the church,' or 'I do all this work for my family at the office.' We boast about, or subtly insert into our conversations, the fact that we are doing a lot of positive and unselfish activity, yet we also may be becoming work addicts or alcoholics (as I did). If the self-justification doesn't work, we just kept doing the pain-relieving behavior to try to feel better.[1]

Going for Help

At this point, if one is wise, he or she may go for counseling. The constructed personality resists 'help' that may reveal its unreality because it would be *mortifying* to be revealed as unreal and a failure! In spite of all the pain and fear, the per-sistent hope is that we will be able to patch up our constructed image. I didn't want to share my fear and pain with a coun-selor because I was baffled and very uneasy (and I felt that with my training and faith I should be able to solve my own problems). But I was a counselor, so I knew I would rec-ommend that someone else in my situation at least talk it over with a therapist. Consciously I was sincere, and I wasn't aware that I had a constructed personality, that I might be out of touch with my reality-evaluator. But at a semiconscious level I was afraid the therapist might see inside me and reveal to me that I really was the self-centered, grandiose person I had been told I was. On the other hand, my hope was that if I was sincere (and I believed that I was), the therapist would vindicate me and see that I had a selfish mate. In other words, without even knowing I had a constructed personality, I went for help hoping that my constructed life as I perceived it would be supported and strengthened.

When my own foundations began to shake and the fear of failure at home got bad enough, I went to counseling for several years for some exploratory 'foundation maintenance.' For some time I thought I was doing well with the therapists with whom I counseled. The tragedy was that, although I was consciously sincere and I always received some help, on at least one occasion I was evidently so smooth in presenting my helping personality that I very subtly got out of the client role by talking about the therapist's vocational issues and dreams of writing. There are some outstanding exceptions of counselors in my life who did not get lured into shifting our therapy sessions onto their own lives and dreams in our counseling, but the insanity of my constructed personality is that this could happen at all.

Trying to Redecorate a Burning House

If a person goes to counseling as a way to 'win' or to get better tools to implement and enforce his or her constructed personality's agenda, then the counseling may bring temporary relief, but probably will not heal the person or free the soul. After a temporary change of behavior in the one being counseled, the constructed personality will feel stronger and almost surely reassert itself, the conflict will return in some form, and the basic relationship warfare will continue. Such patch-up changes are just damage-control behaviors added to our arsenal of performance-oriented activities to shore up the crumbling, frightened constructed personality.

The old controlling patterns will reappear after counseling *unless* our denial cracks open somehow, and we become willing to face ourselves and our constructed lives. For authentic spiritual healing to occur, counseling must relate to the issues of the inner warfare: the denial, the self-centeredness of the constructed personality, and its inappropriate tendency to play God and control people, places, and things to get its own way.

Sometimes a family member or a boss will try to force a person who is in denial with an out-of-control constructed self to go to counseling or treatment. But one person – a spouse or friend – forcing a dysfunctional person to go to counseling to patch things up without that person *wanting* help seldom works, though it may appear to. Sometimes this one-on-one intervention may lead to more misery for everyone.[2]

I remember a story I heard years ago about a three-year-old child whose mother was trying to get him to sit down in his high chair. He had his legs stiff, and he was resisting greatly.

The mother said, 'I told you, sit down in the high chair. Sit down! Sit! You're going to sit.'

'No, no, no!' was the stubborn response.

'Sit down in that high chair!' said the mother once more. Then she swept his feet out from under him and plopped him into the chair, saying, 'You *are* sitting down now, see?'

The child glowered and said, 'I may be sitting down outside, but inside I'm still standing up.'

I think a lot of us go to counseling that way. We come out 'looking like' we've been counseled and saying appropriate things because the constructed personality is very clever. But our constructed self is still standing up on the inside. Participating in counseling this way is very self-defeating and shortsighted. A dear friend pointed out, 'It's like wetting your pants to get warm.' We may even do this sort of avoidance-counseling sincerely, which is really baffling. I was consciously very serious about searching for truth, and still my life cratered.

When going to counseling doesn't solve the problems, the pain, fear, and loneliness experienced can be absolutely horrifying. It's like a free fall through the darkness alone. During its fall the constructed personality is looking anywhere and everywhere for some way, some parachute – or some person – to save its constructed life!

Remember, our constructed personalities were put together in the beginning by a frightened child to fend off fear and shame, much of which had been introjected from adults. For years that fear and shame may have been kept at bay by the successful performance of the constructed personality. But now, all the early fear and shame come roaring back. The struggle to keep things in control and to deny the growing reality that failure is looming on all levels is excruciating. We seem to be caught in a whirlwind of broken pieces of our lives and sucked into the spiraling black hole of failure and rejection as important people start turning their backs, backing away, or jumping ship entirely.

Finally the pain caused by the compulsive or addictive escape behaviors one engages in while trying to medicate or alleviate the pain and fear make the medication more painful than the disease. We quit enjoying the drinking, eating, work, compulsive religious activities, or whatever behaviors or compulsions we have taken up to quiet the pain and fear.

However long it takes to play itself out, sooner or later a

devastating personal and/or vocational crisis may loom. This is where the drama gets very complicated, and the fear and loneliness are numbing.

The Soul's Darkest Moment

Maybe you discover that you're on the brink of losing your job, or you are faced with an imminent divorce; whatever it is, a definite crisis may arrive when the constructed life is about to lose something it's afraid to face life without. All of a sudden you are threatened with a kind of intolerable exposure, perhaps a public one, with the unmistakable failure of the constructed personality. God seems to be a million miles away. The words of prayer are cold sawdust in the mouth.

When you're about to lose something that seems irreplaceable in your life's bet for success, self-esteem, and love, it feels like you are being impelled inexorably toward the abyss. For many, this loss of the hope of success, or vocation, or relationship survival leads to a certain kind of depression that is very common in America – a solitary inner sense of lostness and lack of energy or compelling purpose to go on that is experienced as a choking darkness by the imprisoned soul.

Is There No Hope?

You may be thinking, 'Does everyone fail? What about people whose constructed personalities succeed and they become wealthy, famous, or great political or religious leaders? Did they beat the odds?'

Of course those are good questions. But as one who has counseled with such people, I have discovered that even the big winners sometimes have the same failures on the inner journey if they have locked up their reality-measuring souls.

Let's say that instead of failing, our constructed life succeeds and wins a great deal of approval and esteem for us. The surprising tragedy about this outcome is that, for the constructed personality in denial, even super fame and approval are seldom enough to bring the self-esteem and love we feel we must have. Success may even add a new fear that the individuals will lose what they have now gained. In any case, the esteem received from material success is time-limited in nature, often dissipating quickly.

The first time this happened to me was early in my attempts at constructing a winning personality. I remember an April night in 1945. I was a senior at Tulsa Central High School, and it was the biggest night of my eighteen-year-old life. I had been elected king of the school, and they had just announced the results to the three candidates. It was the night of the 'coronation,' and I was in my crown and robe, sitting on a bar stool backstage alone, waiting for the trumpets and drum roll.

As I waited, I had some strange and surprising thoughts. Being king was just the final affirmation in a string of high school successes – senior class president, part of a basketball team undefeated in regular season, a lead in the class play, winner of a dramatic reading contest, and a member of a special men's social club. I couldn't believe I was the one to whom all these things had happened. I should have been ecstatic – but I wasn't.

I was surprised then that a part of me wasn't even touched by all that had happened. I realize now the part that was numb was the most important part of me, my introverted soul. No wonder I couldn't feel the joy and wonder of all those special honors. I sensed that I didn't deserve them – that my constructed personality had done it all to get the success that would make me feel good about myself so my dad would love me. Yet I was afraid to look out in the audience to see if my father had even come to see my 'coronation.' Inside, my shaming voices were telling me I didn't deserve to be there, that I was a phony because I spoke to everyone in the hall by name, even those who seemed to have no friends. My voices said I was just a politician. Suddenly I felt very old, tired, and self-conscious.

As the trumpets blared the triumphant entry signal and I stood up, my last thought was, 'Is this all there is? Isn't success supposed to feel better?' I opened the door and smiled into the blinding bright lights.

Here's the catch: the shaming voices are relentless, and continue to make us miserable, even when our constructed personality has been very successful! Sin and evil are notoriously patient and insidious as they slip invisibly into the cracks caused by our self-centered choices and spoil our happiness. Because the constructed person has assumed that success would bring peace and esteem, he or she may look in the mirror one morning after a glorious success and hear the shaming voices say, 'You think you're something? Ha! You're really nothing!' 'You're dumb!' 'You're too fat.' 'You're too thin.' 'Your nose is still too big.' Or 'Your ears stick out. And now you're old and getting flabby!' 'You don't even deserve to be successful. If people really knew you, they wouldn't even want to be associated with you!'

The sarcastic voices tell us that we are not really competent – even if we direct a large corporation or are movie stars, great athletes, religious leaders, or heads of state. The shaming voices keep hammering on the foundation of our constructed lives, and they can cause serious cracks as they periodically remind us of all the things that we started out feeling insecure about and that seemed wrong with us. When we make a normal mistake, even at the height of success, they say, 'You sorry so and so. At your stage in life you're *still* doing it wrong, aren't you? Will you *ever* get it right?' Even when we are sixty-five or even eighty-five years old, the voices can still torment us.

During all of this process the universal bent to control and be number one, promoted by Sin and the patient presence of evil, tempts us to take moral shortcuts to win big and gain more esteem out there in the world. Both of these unseen adversarial forces urge additional and often self-defeating action to try to shore up our still fragile and insufficient self-esteem.

When confronted with the strength and pain of the rejecting shaming voices and the loss of their reality-orienting souls, even very successful people often cannot perceive the positive reality in their lives at the height of their success or see any way to redeem their lives. Some even commit suicide. Though the imprisoned soul cries out in the night for us to give up trying to get self-esteem through success or 'goodness,' we have to learn through painful experience that external success just does not bring the basic self-esteem for which we yearn.

We realize we have misunderstood what the game of life is all about. We 'bet everything on the wrong horse' when it came to meeting the needs for love and self-esteem. When success turns out to be hollow, the successful person, like those who have failed unmistakably, may go into a self-defeating control mode, alienate those around her or him, and eventually have to face powerlessness and a depressive sense of failure before healing can be found. Even when the constructed personality gets everything it wanted, it still may 'foul its own nest.' That's evidently a part of our basic bent toward control and self-centered perfectionism called Sin.

I believe many highly acclaimed successful people such as movie stars, super athletes, bank presidents, and others become victims of alcoholism and other addictions, or commit suicide after they achieve their greatest successes because they believe the shaming voices' irrational, shaming, negative evaluations of the reality of their situation. They can't assimilate the magnitude or reality of their outward success accurately because they have locked away their reality-measuring soul. Since they feel like failures, they may unconsciously bring about the destruction of their tortured constructed personality.

Amazingly these self-defeating tragedies – if not fatal – may contain the seeds of good news.

At the Spiritual Crossroads

We are now at one of the most difficult crossroads in the human spiritual journey toward reality and God. As long as we think our constructed personality is capable of saving us, we have unwittingly made our constructed selves God. And since our constructed personality cannot save us, we have set ourselves up for certain ultimate failure.

This is another of the many paradoxes of faith: God's strength really does come through the awareness of our own weakness. It's not that we must lose everything we have and experience a crisis that absolutely destroys the constructed personality. Evidently, we must see and own the fact that all our constructed ability, charm, and effort cannot 'make it all right,' 'save us,' or give us the sense of self-esteem and love that the constructed life was built to bring home. Only when we recognize that we can't save ourselves does the constructed person discover perhaps the greatest paradox of the soul's adventure: *spiritual healing and strength begin with the admission of powerlessness*! Knowing this is hard enough, but stepping across the threshold of failure and *admitting* we are powerless may be humankind's most difficult spiritual step.

Yet it is at this point that we are most open to being touched by the healing hand of God.

12

Conversion: God to the Rescue?

SOME TIME DURING THIS DEPRESSING FEARFUL STRUGGLE THAT seems to be the end of the line in the inner adventure, the idea may be introduced to our floundering constructed personality that we can get help by a personal commitment of our lives to God. Although we may have believed in God for years, the idea of actually turning over the authority and outcome of our lives to God is a new notion for the constructed personality because, in a practical sense, *it* has become the god of our lives.

This may seem strange, but in the spiritual realm – operationally – our god and our idols are not what we *say* they are but what we *obey* (see Matt. 7:21–27). This is true whether that reigning 'god' is the love of money, a child, one's work, alcohol, sex, or the constructed personality built to gain the self-esteem that only God can give. So one's idol may be whatever the hottest focus of one's life is – that to which he or she gives the highest priority in matters requiring time and attention. Since the constructed personality becomes the chief operating officer of our lives who rationalizes and enables these lesser idols, the constructed self *is* our god operationally.

The Shaming Voices Can Set Our Spiritual Agenda

Over the years the shaming voices become like abusive parents whom children hate, but obey when they build lives in opposition to their mother and father. Then, ironically, the children wind up being much like those hated parents. I remember talking with a group of men at a picnic. One of the men's sons, a little boy, was raising cane, pushing girls down and running away laughing. His harried mother finally dragged the boy over to his father for correction. The father grabbed the boy, shouted an obscenity at him while shaking him hard enough to rattle his teeth, and gave him what sounded like a death threat if he didn't 'straighten up.' The father then shoved his son back toward the other children. The boy stumbled over a rock and fell as his father came back into our group. Behind the father's back I saw the boy mouth the words, 'I hate you!' The father, shaking his head and chuckling, said, 'I don't know what's the matter with that kid. He's out of control – just like his mother.'

We looked at the father but said nothing. It seemed obvious that the boy was a carbon copy of the father he'd expressed hatred for.

Instead of our honest, loving, God-directed soul guiding us, the shaming voices have dominated our lives and relationships and, in a sense, forced us to build the skewed constructed personality that then takes over and becomes the controlling false god on whom we count to save us.

This awareness – that many of my decisions I had thought were being made to do God's will were in fact made to quiet the shaming voices and gain self-esteem – has helped me see how my own life has been twisted and distorted by my constructed personality's attempts to get esteem to counteract the negative messages of the shaming voices. This experience of human blindness as to my own motives has helped make clear what the biblical good news means in a contemporary world when Jesus said, in effect, that God had come in Him to give us sight in our blindness – the ability to see what's real – to free us from the prisons of shame, guilt, and brokenness caused by our out-of-control, self-centered lives (see Luke 4:16–21).

How Do People Find Out About Getting Help From God?

People hear about God and being saved in all sorts of ways but often they aren't listening until their own lives get very shaky. One day in that lonely, shut down, crumbling life, a floundering man or woman may meet a different sort of person, someone who appears to be filled with life and integrity, who is talking about God in a different way – about a personal relationship with God. Suddenly that clear-speaking stranger re-triggers the childhood yearnings for a perfect parent (see chapter 4). The searcher has what appears to be a whole new attraction and rush of energy for God.

The idea of getting help from God can come from all sorts of situations: as a result of somebody getting up and giving a witness about finding hope in a relationship with God; from people telling their stories of finding new life on the brink of death in a twelve-step group; from hearing a sermon or a counselor; from going to a class at church; from reading a book; or from meeting a spiritual person filled with love and hope. Somehow we grasp the idea, 'Maybe my life can change! Maybe I can get out from under this lonely, hopeless charade!' And when such an idea makes a solid landing in one's mind, that person has a glimmer of hope that God just might be real.

But that hope immediately leads to the most intense trouble yet: when the suggestion is presented to the constructed person that commitment to God is the way to relief, the constructed personality may go ballistic in its resistance and reject the person bringing such a bizarre message, along with the message itself. At this point the interior battle is often experienced as a serious struggle: the imprisoned soul shouts faintly from its prison, pleading for the individual to face reality and surrender to God. On the other hand, the constructed personality argues, almost from its grave, for the independence of our false (but familiar) constructed life as it is. The constructed personality says, 'No way I'm going to give up control! I can handle this alone! Things are not that bad!'

When the idea becomes conscious that you may be approaching the possibility of surrendering your life and future to God, you may suddenly get an enormous amount of ridicule from the shaming voices (as well as others you talk to) who may make fun of the idea. The voices may say things like, 'Aw, isn't it sweet? Now you're going to be a holy person, you're going to be a weak little saint. Remember pious old Aunt Nell? Everybody laughed at her behind her back. Well, they'll be laughing at you too!'

Or if you're a very rational, scientific kind of person, the voices might say, 'This is not logical. It is ridiculous and naive that you should turn control of your life over to God. Even if there were a God, copping out by giving up responsibility of your life is intellectually irresponsible. The whole idea is a perfect example of the power of delusion and the naive longing for an unhealthy dependence.' Or you may have a wave of fear that if you make such a surrender, you'll never be able to get any self-esteem. You'll just be a nonrespected religious wimp!

So regardless of the stance of our constructed personality and its defenses (strong or weak), there's almost a universal resistance to admitting powerlessness and 'giving up' or surrendering to *anyone* – perhaps especially to God. We fear that people will think we're incompetent or ignorant or weak if we commit our lives to God, and that we'll lose any hope for self-esteem we might still have after our failure.

Still the persistent soul cries out from prison, 'You need help! Facing the truth can make you *free*! The reality is that you are about to go under! You are *powerless* to stop the destruction!' Right in the middle of the inner war the constructed personality feels that it is being choked to death. This battle is very serious business. It's the struggle for the spiritual survival of the only life we know at the moment – our trembling constructed personality.

Thomas Gordon said years ago, 'There seems to be something in human nature, whether learned or acquired, rooted in the organic make-up of all organisms, something that predisposes us to defend our world of reality, however false it may be against the threat of change.'[1] We're dealing with the bottom-line vulnerability of human experience, our fear of change and losing control!

'Conversion' of the Constructed Personality

When the pain and fear of the constructed personality gets intense enough, we may finally be open to getting help from outside. Let's say that a Christian we meet at this point tells us that if we make a personal commitment or surrender to God, then God will help solve our problems.

My mother taught me the Lord's Prayer when I was a child, and since that time I've known that for me Christianity is very important. If that was part of your early life, then when you are standing on the brink of the abyss, you may hear from somewhere that the only help left will come through a certain kind of 'personal relationship with Jesus.' You are told that you can get healed from your agony through a commitment of your whole life to God in Jesus Christ.

So when the wheels are coming off the constructed personality and we invite God to come into our life and save us, God seems to take us – whatever our motives are when we come. As the hymn says, we come 'just as I am without one plea.' God will accept whatever step we make toward Him. Therefore if it's our constructed personality that moves toward God to get freed, God will take that.

You may have thought that getting changed through a commitment of your life to God in Jesus Christ was naive, as I did when I was growing up. I just didn't think that you could really get help with your very personal issues that way. I was 'too smart' for that. Believing in God and praying to Him the way I already did was enough. Then when I was about thirty years old, life got so painful that something had to change.

Everyone in my immediate family had died in the previous few years; I'd held their hands at the last and heard their last words or confessions (at least my mother's and father's – my only brother was killed in a plane crash as an Air Force pilot in August 1945, fifteen days before the Second World War was over). After serving in the Navy I had finished college in 1950 and gone into the oil exploration business. Then in 1952 I went to seminary as a layman to try to understand about God and life, but left after two years. The sense of failure because I had left the seminary was excruciating. I'd made good grades but did not feel called to be ordained.

When I came back to the oil exploration business, where I'd worked since I graduated from college, there was no way I could explain to the people around me what was going on inside my life. Behind the confident personality I had constructed was a lot of pain and fear, and a realization that I didn't know who I was or what I was supposed to do with my life. I had a wife I loved very much and two babies I loved deeply. But there seemed to be no hope, no ultimate purpose any more. I'd thought being a minister would give me the fulfillment I longed for. If there was a God, the people at the seminary had subtly hinted that I must have turned away from Him when I left and didn't choose to be ordained (or perhaps this was my imagination?). At any rate, I felt things closing in on me in the inner chamber of my life. My constructed world was badly damaged and I did not know where to turn.

One day, in August 1956, as I was driving through the pine woods country of East Texas, I suddenly pulled off the road and stopped in a grove of tall pine trees. I remember sitting there in almost complete despair. I was like a man on a great gray treadmill going no place, in a world that was made up of black, black clouds all around me. My constructed personality had failed to get the success and esteem I'd felt sure it could.

As I sat there, I began to weep like a little boy, which I suddenly realized I was – inside. I looked up toward the sky. There was nothing I wanted to do with my life. The cracks in my constructed self were threatening to split me apart and destroy me. I turned to God in my mind and said simply, *'God, if there's anything you want in this stinking soul, take it.'*

That was years ago. But something came into my life that

day that I really needed: hope. As I sat there by the roadside, I continued to cry, only now the tears were a release from a lifetime of being bound by myself, by the terrific drive to prove that I was something. What that something was I would not understand until twenty years later.

I started the car and turned toward home.

I began to read everything I could about conversion, and what I had experienced seemed to be almost classic. I had given as much of my life as I could to as much of God as I could understand. I worked very hard for the next few years to be the best Christian anywhere, and went thousands of miles across the world to tell people there was hope in Christ. Therefore I didn't understand why, after some exciting years, the feelings of insecurity, my lack of self-esteem, and my compulsive working habits came storming back, haunting my Christian experience as they had my secular life: my old compulsive need for self-esteem was raising its head once more. How could this be, when I was converted and had asked God to fill me with His spirit? Later, after years of anguish and trying to fix myself, I would see how my *constructed personality* had latched on to the conversion experience and locked my soul back in prison as I went back to work to be a *star – this time for God!*

Religious Commitment Without the Soul

When people commit their lives to Christ in this way, they become Christians. There's no question in my mind about that. But it is also possible to get the unreal life repaired and still be cut off from the soul, which remains in prison.

It seems to work like this: We make this commitment, perhaps, because our marriage isn't good, or our business is going down the drain, and we feel great stress. We turn to God, hoping that God will save or improve these things. We are stepping into God's family in good faith. Many people have a wonderful experience of grace as I did, a sense of freedom from the fear and guilt that had plagued me. I was as sincere as I could be; I don't discount that experience at all. But what I want to tell you now is that I woke up one day to discover something shocking!

The constructed personality can make a commitment to Jesus Christ and sincerely adopt the Christian behaviors of converted people: Bible study, prayer, worship, loving people for Christ's sake, tithing, even talking to people about giving their lives to Christ, as I did as director of a place called Laity Lodge. But this next part of what I want to tell you was so subtle and frightening to me that I want to say it as clearly as I can.

The constructed personality may have felt defeated and sincerely entered the Christian life, but the constructed self may not have given up on the constructed personality's agenda to go out in the world and get love and esteem! The constructed personality may sincerely take on the behavior of a whole committed Christian lifestyle, still not realizing that inside, the constructed personality still thinks love and self-esteem will come from outside – but now it will come through all these new Christian friends and works he or she is doing. The only difference is that now we are unconsciously depending on success in the 'Christian world' to bring us esteem and love, instead of success in the business world or whatever vocational or personal worlds we had been counting on before our personal commitment.

In fact, many of us *do* get real relief and esteem from others at this point. Other church members will love us if we commit our lives to Christ and love them. Some people we try to help outside the church will esteem us. This wonderful and real relief combined with the acceptance and love received from good people appear at first to be the total experience of grace people have always talked about, the birth of a new spiritual personality.

However, if we surrender to Christ for the purpose of patching up our constructed life, this happy experience of relief may be the joy felt by the constructed personality who once more didn't get destroyed. 'Whew! We made it again!' We have had our neck saved and our constructed life restored – along with our original agenda to get love and esteem out there, except now we've got the whole church and God to help us.

I've come to realize that it was actually my constructed personality that I surrendered to God on that roadside – for a new chance. The evidence for me is that although I *said* I had trusted God with my life, after a honeymoon period of several years, I didn't have self-esteem, I could not give up control of that new life of ministering to God, and I was still very much afraid of failing. I wanted *help* from God to run that life and ministry, and I thought that was what I needed from God, some 'help.' When I feared failure, I said sincerely, 'I surrender it to You.' But my continued fear and performance anxiety should have told me that I *really* wanted God to be 'Our Consultant-assistant who art in Heaven.' So, when I had failed to get love and esteem as a controlling male businessperson, I turned that constructed personality over to Christ, and before long I became a controlling male *Christian* businessperson with a lot of good works and applause under his belt.

Although my friends and my activities changed drastically, from a preoccupation with succeeding in business to 'doing God's work,' nothing had changed with regard to my goal: I was still trying to control people, places, and things to assure the successful outcome of my ministry. I could not see this because I still had my reality-checking soul locked in its prison. I was still trying to get esteem and love through success in my work, my ministry 'out there' with my constructed personality.

I believe that God offers incredible love and esteem without cost or strings attached, but I evidently wasn't willing to accept them from God as a free gift. That was too easy – and I couldn't control it. Although most of this was not conscious at that time, my actions revealed that I wanted to maintain control and deserve esteem from God and from the Christian world by doing God's work – and doing it very well. I had no idea that, although I had committed my constructed personality to God for His healing and help, I hadn't surrendered my soul or my constructed life's goals at all.

'Do You Know the Peace of God?'

Many good people make a commitment to Christ, join the church, and get on a busy, exciting, religious adventure. I'm not saying, of course, that such people are not Christians or that they lack integrity. But I am saying that often many of them are on a *religious* journey rather than a *spiritual* one. They learn everything they can about the Bible, doctrine, the order of service, and the history of the church. They join study groups, pray, teach, tithe, serve on committees, evangelize other people, and even get ordained, but they are still over-committed and miserable in their personal relationships, feel inadequate inside, and are fearful about the success of their performance in life! I am convinced that God accepts us, loves us, and relates to us in our constructed personalities even if we are dominated by a relentless drive to earn the esteem and liberty God wants to give us freely. But it's sad to do it this way, and after a while it's not much fun.

After my conversion by the roadside, I did most of those religious behaviors listed above and even went back to seminary and got a degree. But I was miserable and baffled because I was working so hard to succeed in seminary. It is obvious to me now that if we do become Christians to save our unreal constructed personality, it will not necessarily bring the spiritual healing and esteem our feelings are crying out for. We are, in effect, asking God to bless our unreal lives, our manipulative and nontrusting means of getting self-esteem. True spiritual healing, however, brings the ability to receive self-love and self-esteem *from within* so that we don't have to depend on manipulating people, pleasing them, succeeding as Christians, or buttering others up in order to get them to give us that esteem and the freedom true spiritual healing brings.

Remember, the soul seeks and demands a spiritual, or *real*, connection with God, with people, with ourselves and our motives, and with vocational choices. I have no doubt that God accepts those who come to Him with constructed personalities. We all seem to build them. But by the nature of reality and intimacy, a constructed person cannot have the intimate and spiritual relationship with God that the soul cries out for because the constructed personality is not real. Spiritually, reality and unreality evidently cannot mix (see 1 John 1:5–6).[2]

The Transition: From Religious to Spiritual

If we have moved through the ridicule and resistance of the shaming voices and the resistances of the constructed personality and made a serious commitment to God, even if it is only a commitment of the constructed personality, we may experience hope and temporary relief at finding a way to avoid destruction. But sooner or later, if we are fortunate, a new kind of struggle may begin, an even more fearful struggle: we face the change that can release the soul from its prison and lead us toward creative freedom and the tools to bring peace in our own homes.

Part 3

Prison Break: God Springs the Soul!

13

How Converted People Can Fail: The Elephant in the Sanctuary Nobody Mentions

WHEN THE SERIOUS COMMITMENT TO GOD RESTORES AND strengthens the constructed personality, things often work out very well for a while, sometimes even for years, as people change secular habits for religious ones. This initially exciting experience of happy relief and the improvement in life is so common that people have called it the 'honeymoon period' of commitment. During this time some decide to become full-time church or social workers or even ordained ministers. Yet for many people, when the honeymoon is over, the constructed personality jumps back in control and the inner stress and lack of self-worth return, even though the person is consciously still committed to God.

Last year I talked with a minister of a large church who said, 'I made a commitment of my life to Christ eight years ago, and I am now the senior pastor of the largest church in the state in my denomination. Yet I never feel like I've done enough, and I'm plagued by self-doubts and fears about my marriage and how I'm going to get everything done. Many of my fellow ministers say they envy me, but in the privacy of my own heart that seems to me like a bad joke. I'm a converted Christian who's supposed to feel peace and joy, but secretly I feel exhausted and confused. I've got a great ministry, but I don't know where my life disappeared to.'

If you don't think this is a common problem for converted Christians, check around in the church.

Churches Can Foster Conversions of the Constructed Personality

A sad situation in the Christian community is that some churches have many members or even pastors who are hard-working, moral people whose reality-oriented souls are virtually untouched by their serious and sincere religious beliefs. These churches become the friend of religion and of society, but they can become the enemy of the soul on the spiritual adventure. They affirm a life of religious activities without relating these activities to issues of character and integrity. Indeed they may never connect religious faith to dishonesty with one's self (denial), control, using people, competition, gossiping, judging, and political manipulation to get one's way. In short, these churches promote living a 'religious' life without dealing with an individual's reality-oriented inner life that demands the dismantling of their personal constructed personality's agenda (which may even coincide with the present agenda of their church as well).

The *soul's* search is for reality, love, integrity, freedom from bondage, forgiveness, and God. This spiritual journey is what

Jesus lived and taught about, as did most of the Hebrew prophets. The call was not, 'Come to church and worship, study about God, and give tithes.' The Pharisees did that with great conscientiousness. Jesus' call, paraphrased, was to 'follow me and quit giving precedence to your old life' (see Matt. 10:37–39). 'And as you learn what I'm teaching, you'll find the truth that will free you' (see John 8:31–32). We are to learn to live using the way Jesus lived as our model: first of all to be honest; to give and receive love, forgiveness, and healing; and to enjoy living and serving God as a nondefensive servant on the threatening playing fields of life.

As we do these things, we are trusting God (not skillful, clever manipulation) for the *outcome* of our efforts. In my case I had to discover that the manipulating, ambitious constructed personality – with its intense focus on getting love and esteem through superior performance – would not help me live the soul's adventure, even in the church. I had to do more good things than others did and do them perfectly, so unless people were in trouble and needed counseling, I had trouble taking the time to relax and hang out with them to hear the dreams of their souls. I was too busy succeeding in doing God's work.

Jesus hit this use of religious behavior to gain esteem very hard. He talked about how we must give up trying to be the best, the first, the most honored (see Matt. 20:25–28 and John 13:2–15). He told the Pharisees that even though they were very committed to God, they were religious 'whited sepulchers' (Matt. 23:27, KJV), constructed personalities who looked good and spiritual on the outside, but inside were unreal and cunning, using religious behaviors to manipulate esteem from others. Though they were on all the religious talk shows and best-seller lists, Jesus said that inside they were rotting like dead men's bones.

One day I realized why the Pharisees got so angry about what Jesus said: they were in such denial that they probably didn't even know they were doing those things he accused them of – just like me.

'I Tried God, But It Didn't Work'

So, what if we commit our lives to God and the initial sense of relief and hope ebbs away in a few years? We often don't see that many of us in the church *talk* about the freedom of Christ, yet we are amazingly compulsive and fearful, not free or loving and forgiving in our daily lives. With all our success, many of us have lost the sense of being loved and of self-esteem. When that happens, we're in big trouble. We are really helpless: we have tried God and done everything the church asked of us, and it still 'didn't work' to bring the peace, happiness, and fulfillment that we understood Jesus *promised*! If and when that happens, we may experience one of two responses.

DROPPING OUT

Apparently thousands of people have responded to the apparent failure of their conversion experience by dropping out of the church because it just 'didn't work' for them. These people were inwardly miserable even though they were converted, active in the church, and sometimes had asked for the 'filling of the Holy Spirit.'

Years ago a huge international evangelistic organization said that by 1990 the whole world would be converted. Obviously we haven't made it, but if everybody who made a commitment to God had freed their souls, found authentic hope in a new life, and kept facing their unreality and growing spiritually, the numbers – and certainly the influence of the church – might be substantially greater than they are.

SWITCH TO RELIGIOUS AMBITION

Other people choose another response to the decline of happiness and relief after the 'honeymoon' (besides dropping out of church). These committed constructed people make a deep internal transfer and say, 'Lord, I believe that You are real and I have hope, so I'm really going to go to work for You!' Such people may become the pillars of their churches and sometimes even their denominations.

When the conversion honeymoon feelings were over for me, I said, 'Lord, I hear You calling me, so I'm going to be the best Christian lay person You've got!' Without knowing it, I entered a kind of competition that felt strangely like the same kind of competition I'd experienced in business. If you're a lay person and this is the route you choose, you may work very consciously to have a bigger lay ministry. If you're a minister, you may go after larger churches or try to get more people. If you lead a nonprofit ministry or are a denominational official, you might go after having greater authority or becoming more outstanding somehow – for Christ.

All this may sound normal and healthy on the surface – and it may well be for some. But others (as in my case) make the unconscious switch of the constructed personality's focus and work from trying to get feelings of self-esteem through secular success to trying to get self-esteem through successful religious behavior.

Because this deception with one's self about who or what one is truly serving is usually not fully conscious to the constructed person, the problem is difficult to diagnose in ourselves – although ironically, it is pretty easy to see in others. (See reference to the 'mote and the beam,' Matt. 7:3, KJV.)

One way to test whether this self-deception has happened to you as a Christian – to determine if you are still controlled by your constructed personality – is to ask the following questions:

- Although I have sincerely committed my life to God, am I still stressed and accused of being controlling?
- Do my spouse or children think I am insensitive and overcommitted?
- Are there signs that my spouse or associates think I am grandiose and in denial?
- Am I insecure about my lack of self-esteem – evidenced by my high performance anxiety?
- Am I still inordinately afraid of failure?
- Am I not as close to my spouse or family as I once was?
- Have I forgotten the dreams of intimacy with them and the dreams of creativity I once cherished?
- Am I more than a little conscious of what people think of me (my clothes, car, house, position, or success)?

Although these are pretty common experiences among high-achieving Americans generally, I'm talking about Christians who say they have surrendered their lives to God in Jesus Christ and now trust Him! For us, these are some of the signs that our reality-seeking souls are imprisoned, that we are still controlled by our constructed personalities.

The response of 'going to work to be the best Christian' may account for many of the addictive and compulsive traits that have surfaced in Christians and in Christian leaders over the last few years, certainly in my life. This is true because sooner or later, a life, even a 'committed Christian life,' that is not connected to and guided by the reality-seeking soul may defeat itself. That tendency is part of what Sin is all about. The constructed person may keep working compulsively until illness or death allows him or her to rest. Or the compulsive work will continue to escalate until a new crisis, rejection, or moral failure is generated by the control attempts of that compulsive person who is living out the 'Outstanding Christian' syndrome.

My own experience of creating this crisis may help clarify some of the subtlety, tragedy, and possible hope to be discovered in this strange aberration of the 'committed Christian life.' But first, let's take a look at the change that *can* free the soul, and how that change can take place!

14

Life-Changing Experience that Frees the Soul

THE INTERNAL STRUGGLE TO PATCH UP A LIFE – EVEN A Christian life – may last for years. But the kind of spiritual experience that finally frees the soul from its prison cell often seems to require a much more profound crisis than just being afraid we may fail in some area or areas of our lives! In the profound kind of conversion I'm about to describe, our constructed personality (and/or our Christian constructed personality) is absolutely at the end of its rope. We face a cataclysmic crisis with which we feel we *cannot* cope. We are paralyzed, and we experience our constructed life crashing and burning around us.

Perhaps this disintegration starts when someone we love and depended on dies, or we get a divorce, or we get involved in some kind of scandal that we feel we cannot face when it is discovered. Perhaps we are struck with a physical disability – as the apostle Paul was struck blind (Acts 9:1–9). When we come to the end of our best strategies to get things under control, there may be a moment when we are in the eye of the hurricane, waiting for we-don't-know what. In that moment we know that we're at a new place of fear – and we may not survive.

Paradoxically, through this kind of seemingly ultimate failure and helplessness may come a spiritual cataclysm that can free the soul. God's power really is made perfect in our weakness (see 2 Cor. 12:9). This spiritual change and its consequences in one's inner life involve something quite different from what one experiences when he or she responds to the gospel with a personal commitment because of a cognitive, rational decision, or as a result of being discouraged, or because he or she hopes that God will revive a business or a relationship before it's too late.

Facing our Powerlessness as the Truth

The spiritual search takes on a whole new direction and a new quality of uncertainty. We're not trying to patch up the constructed personality anymore – we know we *can't*. We're not trying to solve specific problems or fix our boss, business, spouse, children, or friends anymore. Now we're trying to *survive* and get out of our pain alive!

Prayers seem to be born frozen or to bounce off the ceiling and crash impotently around us like small hailstones. All our Christian disciplines, like prayer, Bible reading, and communion, don't seem to work to bring peace, love, or hope anymore. We may even have deep doubts as to whether there is anyone out there where we thought God was. And people who have never believed in God are also really scared at this point. This situation constitutes a dramatic spiritual shift!

Now we're starkly aware that we're *powerless*! We've tried everything we know, called in all the help we can think of, and none of it made any difference. We are frightened out of our wits and completely uncertain about the future. We may no longer be blaming others. We are like a drowning person, and we just want help for ourselves *right now*! And yet – even though we seem to be going under for the third time, there is still a secret part of us that doesn't want to surrender or give up and call out for the help we know we must have to survive.

A Glimmer of Hope

When will people consider opening themselves to the surrender of their whole lives and their wills to God in their powerless defeat? Only, it seems, when a new idea comes to mind and we get a flicker of trust that there is really something or someone out there who is powerful enough and dependable enough to handle our whole fouled up life and future, one who loves us and will catch us if we fall. Paul Tournier said that radical spiritual change takes place much like a trapeze artist swinging from one trapeze to another.[1] We hang on with both hands to the old familiar security of the constructed personality as the acrobat hangs from the trapeze. God swings a new security toward us, but jumping for the new security brings the threat of falling into a bottomless abyss. Therefore we try to reach out with one hand and get the new trapeze bar without letting go of the old security of the constructed personality with the other. Unfortunately, it's just too far to reach!

To grow spiritually at this point we must realize that we have no choice. We have to completely turn loose of the old security and jump for the next! That jump is called the 'leap of faith.' In fact, life as spiritual persons is apparently a series of leaps for new securities while letting go of old ones at different levels. The first time we approach the leap of faith toward God regarding our total floundering life, we must really trust that there is a trapeze coming that will support us and move us on toward safety and happiness. We may agonize secretly about this leap through many days, weeks, months, or even years of sleepless nights.

Our wounded constructed personality and shaming voices may join forces to avoid losing control. They may replay in our imaginations, or our dreams, scenes of vocational, personal, or moral failures, imagining that they have been publicly revealed if we surrender to God. We feel that our lives are damaged, almost surely beyond repair, and we're afraid that we will never be happy or serene again. However, when the constructed personality crashes, hits its lowest bottom, a strange thing happens that we could never have predicted: the childlike soul is sprung, *freed from its prison*! It now stands on one side of the crushed constructed life, urging the person toward making the surrender to reality and God!

At this scary, helpless point God has provided a new ally and advocate in the battle, another forceful, articulate, inner voice to counteract the shaming voices. This new voice is that of the clear-eyed newly freed soul. The soul, believing passionately that we can be healed and satisfied by God, begins to clamber out of its crushed cage and tell us: 'Yes, trust me, reality is: God *is* there for *you*!' The soul's cries to us may now have a strong and resonant ring of reality, contrasting with the whines and threats of the shaming voices. Some people at this point may notice that the carefully constructed life never was real, never did really feel right. The soul argues, 'These people with hope in God are right! We need to give it all to God! It's okay, "get up," do it! Surrender, and we'll get a real life!'

Finally, somehow, if we can trust even a little, we come to

believe that there is someone out there beyond our own limited and failed human power and ability, one who has wisdom greater than ours, who actually cares about us, and who can bring us to sanity and peace. When we get to this place, we ache all over from hanging onto the splintered trapeze of the familiar but unsuccessful constructed personality. We still do not know for sure if we're going to fall into total failure or rejection or make it to the trapeze that God is swinging toward us. But now a new kind of hope has been born, and we are not alone inside.

Even if one doesn't believe in God, this strange hope may be born. John Knox, one of this century's greatest theologians, addressed this moment of continuing to reach out beyond our belief – even beyond our hope – on the spiritual adventure. He said, 'What, for example, is the obsession which Gamaleal Bradford describes as a keen, enormous, haunting, never sated thirst for God?'[2] And Bradford was a man who didn't believe in God.

When Francis Thompson tells us of his flight from the 'hound of heaven,' who or what is pursuing him?[3]

When Bertrand Russell cries out that the center of him is always in eternal terrible pain, searching for something beyond what the world contains, what is that something?

When Augustine said, 'Thou has made us for yourself and our souls are restless until we find our rest in Thee,' of whom or what was he speaking?[4]

It is obvious from these remarks made by people in moments of wondering, fear, and loss of confidence in their old security that the word *God* may have the most poignant meaning. This seems to be true even for one who denies God's objective reality. Bertrand Russell said, 'Having spoken of something transfigured, infinite, the beatific vision, God . . . I do not find it. I do not think it is to be found, but the love of it is my life.'[5]

People who have been raised in the church may not understand what I am saying when I talk about believing for the first time that there is a God who can and will help us, since they may have believed in such a God for many years. But even though they may have been sincere believers for a long time, it is often equally difficult for them to *trust* God in a practical sense in this seemingly ultimate crisis of their constructed personalities – in the face of the agonizing fear generated by a huge problem that threatens their reputation, relationships, financial ruin, or entire future well-being. They may be surprised and horrified to see that they too have a constructed faith that vanishes in the face of real powerlessness.

There is something very deep at the foundation of our lives, our newly emerging soul, that draws us onward in this crucial moment of the search for an authentic experience of trust with God, or ultimate reality. But we still may be truly afraid. If we've been abused badly enough by a parent or a religious person, we can hardly consider moving forward into the leap. Yet our soul deeply wants reality, however great the fear of it or the cost of going for it may be. In the Christian church we call this ultimate reality 'the God of Jesus Christ.' But whatever theological background one comes from, when he or she thinks of surrendering the control of all of her or his life to this awesome being, that person is in a new world of fear.

At the final stage, this inner battle is monumental and often exquisitely frightening as we come toward the surrender that will supposedly lead to freedom and a new life. Our question has moved from 'Are we going to get help from God to get our lives back on track?' to, 'Are we going to surrender the *whole show*, our entire future, to God and not know where it will lead?' This can be an absolutely terrifying thing to almost anybody who understands what he or she is doing. But at this point the constructed personality is hanging in pieces.

Suddenly the entire climate of the secret inner adventure can get very chaotic and anxious. The shaming voices seem to realize that their lives are in danger too. They may mount a stupendous emotional multimedia blitz to stop the movement toward surrender. They do this because they seem to know that if the newly humbled person and the soul join forces and surrender totally to God, it will be the beginning of the end of the shaming voices' control of that individual and of their reign as god-maker in his or her life.

The caustic shaming comments about the loss of face in surrendering may increase until the failed constructed person feels stretched to the breaking point between those shaming voices and the strong calling of the newly freed soul to surrender to God. Many people can't stand the tension of this struggle. They may run away from home, get blind drunk, have affairs, or do whatever they can to try to escape both the messengers who are carrying this insane message about surrender and the constructed personality's painful urging to do the seemingly impossible and 'Hang in there and never give up! Stay in control! Fix it yourself.'

Support from God: Resurgence of the Guidance System Yearnings

The small voice saying 'Yes, let's surrender!' seems to be totally outmatched by the shaming voices. But as young and small as the soul's voice is, compared to the veteran adult shaming voices, the sides in the struggle are often more nearly matched than one would think. Remember the four longings that God put in us as children? When a person is at the point of this soul-freeing conversion, one or all of these longings may be re-triggered in the soul, along with their motivational power to move ahead. According to Grant and Miller, all these yearnings were really for God all along:[6]

- The yearning for a perfect parent is the longing for God the Father, which can be truly satisfied only by Him.
- The yearning for perfect companionship is fulfilled in a surrendered relationship with Jesus Christ among His people.
- The yearning for power and freedom is a longing for the Holy Spirit as creative director, strengthener, and teacher.
- The yearning for meaning is the longing for a congruent life of learning, and of receiving and giving love as we try to discover and do God's will.

Whether one is a Christian or not, the point is that from the beginning of our lives, the soul has been connected to and drawn by these strong urges toward reality. When this crisis of trust comes, the now adult person going through this process may realize, 'Good grief, all along there was a design so that when I tried and failed to be god of my own little world, I would reach out for reality in human relationships, and then beyond them to God!'

So once again these yearnings work like magnets and can pull us toward the surrender to God that the soul's small voice is urging us to make.

The Showdown

There has to be a showdown. The confrontation of opposing forces in the inner warfare leads to the personal crisis of the will.[7] We're asked to make a gigantic psychological leap: to acknowledge frankly our sense of unrealness or even worth-lessness, and powerlessness. Ernie Larsen says that, 'Until we are about to lose something we're not prepared to live without, we will not make this surrender.'[8] I agree. In fact, the spiritual transition one makes through this specific surrender to God has been described as a voluntary 'death' experience. But when the moment of surrender comes, what exactly happens? What do we do? What do we say?

15

'Dying' and New Life

Truly, I say to you, unless one is born anew,
he cannot see the kingdom of God.
John 3:3

WHAT DOES IT MEAN TO TALK ABOUT DEATH AND REBIRTH?
The paradoxical notion that it takes a 'death' experience to
enter a new spiritual life is an ancient idea. But my sense of the
Christian or the twelve-step version of this paradox is that we
must die to our old life, our unreal constructed personality
with its grandiose and self-glorifying motives, in order to begin
to live fully and creatively the loving, reality-oriented life of
the soul.

How do we take the kind of step that leads to the death
of the shame-dominated controlling constructed personality
and the birth of the 'era of the soul' in our lives? What do we
do or say specifically? The evidence is overwhelming that most
people cannot make such a change at the purely cognitive level.
It seems that we can't just 'decide' intellectually to die to our

constructed life. We can *begin* the process with a conscious decision of the will, but in this surrender we are not just over-coming intellectual resistance; we are up against real power!

Carl Jung talked about this power as something different from cognitive experience. He said that 'in the face of the very real powers that dominate us, only an equally real power can help. No intellectual system, but direct experience only can counterbalance the blind power of our seemingly instinctual course toward self-destruction.'[1]

Jennifer was drinking like an alcoholic. She told me that she was sure she could quit drinking if she would take the time to learn about Alcoholics Anonymous. She said she was going to buy a copy of the 'big book,' *Alcoholics Anonymous*, and study it. One of the most persistent delusions that alcoholics and addicts have is that they can *think* their way into sobriety and overcome the power of alcohol or drugs. Yet most of those who get into recovery and onto a spiritual path learn that recovery is about *power*. The first step is to admit one is 'powerless over alcohol' and that their life 'is unmanageable.' The alcoholic or addict must give up on his or her power in order to find a higher power than himself to counterbalance the blind power driving the individual toward self-destruction.

After several solo attempts at controlled drinking had failed, Jennifer finally saw that she could not quit drinking using her best thinking and most determined willpower. After a great deal more frustration and some serious personal failures, she *finally* relaxed her clinched mind, admitted her powerlessness, and stepped into a new chapter of her healing in which she eventually surrendered her whole life to God. People who have tried to break a compulsion or addiction to overeat, or over-spend, or work compulsively, often have similar stories.

My experience in counseling Christians is that often we too are deluded into thinking we can, by our intellectual grasp of the Bible, the tenets of the faith, and our strength of will, over-come the blind power behind our constructed personality's unremitting course toward self-destruction. The apostle Paul is a classic case. He was brilliant and committed to God, even to the point of killing Christians because of his strong religious convictions. He had to be struck blind before he could experi-ence the humility of powerlessness and enter a spiritual life (see Acts 9).

A Definite, Deliberate Action

I've read literature on conversion experiences for many years. There has been much debate about how a life-changing conversion takes place.[2] A deep conversion is not something we just ooze into by spiritual intention over time. A definite act is apparently necessary.

Dietrich Bonhoeffer, the great German Christian martyr, said, 'Unless a definite step is demanded, the call vanishes into thin air.'[3] How many times have seeking people at the lowest point of their crisis been drawn to surrender their lives to God through a great sermon, a deeply touching story, or a compelling piece of music? Yet if they didn't take any concrete action to respond, the sense of being drawn toward surren-dering to God may have evaporated like a fog in a few hours or after a good night's sleep.

There have been thousands of people who have been deeply changed spiritually without having to 'crash and burn' in what I have described as a dramatic battle. Some have had a long gradual turning toward God, as when a sunflower turns toward the sun.

But I believe that at some time in any one of the many ways of transformation, a moment will come when a person must answer this call to surrender everything before the sorts of changes will occur that can free the soul and reorient the seeking person's life and relationships. My own experience and observation make it difficult to imagine the depth of surrender I'm describing being made peacefully, without a lot of resistance from the shaming voices and the fear of turning loose.

This necessary act is not just saying yes to a proposition. There is within the conversion experience, as in a wedding ceremony, a place to say, 'I do. I commit my life to this joint adventure.' But just as in a wedding, it's a more profound kind of commitment than answering true or false when asked whether we are going to be committed. It is a giving of permission, an agreeing to change, if necessary, our whole personal, sexual, financial, and social lives. A spiritual conversion to God is more of a life surrender than a marriage because it calls us to be willing to obey and change every aspect of our lives to conform to reality as seen in God's will. Even if you have been a very religious person, a deep conversion experience can be quite different, more like opening a door into light or reality on the Godward side of your soul – and walking through it.

John Stott, an Anglican minister and writer, said, 'You can believe in Christ intellectually and admire him. You can say your prayers to him through the keyhole as I did for many years. You can push coins at him under the door. You can be moral, decent and good. You can be religious and pious. You can have been baptized and confirmed. You can be deeply versed in the philosophy of religion. You can be a theological student and even an ordained minister and still not have opened the door of which I am speaking.'[4] There is evidently no substitute for this surrender of the constructed personality and its goals to free the soul.

Yet there is an amazing paradox at the very point of surrender: we are still seeking and yet running from God. Some of us try to run away until the very last step. The tenacity of the constructed personality and the shaming voices to maintain control is *incredible*! Alfred North Whitehead said, 'Until this conflict (between coming toward God and running from Him) is resolved somehow, we cannot make the spiritual movement from God the void to God the friend.'[5] At first we don't even know if He's out there. But then, when God does show up to confront our constructed self, He's the *enemy*. In other words, God's first role in our experience of Him that can lead to surrender is that of the enemy of the constructed personality. At some level we know intuitively that if we give our lives to God, then many behaviors, attitudes, and controlling ways we have relied on for security and the hope for esteem will have to go.

Finally the combination of our pain, combined with the strength of our soul's pleading, the inner yearnings, and the witness of those who have 'tried God,' reach a certain intensity. When that happens, we are ready to move from God the enemy to God the friend.

The Only Way to Win the Battle

John Knox said a spiritual conversion is 'a free and inward giving up of the whole personality to (one we first conceived to be) the enemy, to be captured by the one we started seeking.'[6] God is the reality and love we started seeking as a child in parents, friends, lovers, spouses, and in the search for freedom, meaning, and esteem. It was God who haunted our steps from the time we first reached out for a perfect parent as a baby. God has been tracking this constructed personality of ours and has stayed in touch with our soul at some level all along. These elusive touches may have come through great books, movies, the love of caring people, or touching worship or preaching.

The fortunate person inside a crumbled constructed personality realizes for a blessed instant that the only way possible to be victorious in this struggle is to surrender, to give it all up, to submit to God in a complete offering of ourselves. For as we do this, in some mysterious way, the soul becomes connected to God like a space capsule docking into its base. With that connection made, the soul is not only free from the solitary prison of silence, it can also receive the continuing spiritual strength it will need to replace the constructed personality as the individual's guide to fulfillment in the reality that is God's will.

This freeing experience ushers in the beginning steps in what appear to be personal miracles, like ceasing to hide behind our pretensions of being super strong, smart, beautiful, or right in order to get the esteem and love we are seeking. God's offer to the soul is to give us that love, strength, and wisdom we have sought so frantically to earn in order to win the esteem and fulfillment, the lack of which may have haunted our every decision. No wonder people feel victorious after surrendering to God. Their constructed personalities have lost, but *they* have won! They are free from having to run from God and reality (which, because God is everywhere, makes it an impossibly long run).

The Moment of Surrender is Hard to Describe

Here are statements of some of the historically great souls at the moment of surrender. Thomas à Kempis, who lived in the thirteenth century and wrote *The Imitation of Christ*, a book probably read by more people than any book about Christianity except the Bible, said in surrendering, 'Oh Lord, all things that are in heaven and earth are thine. I desire to offer myself to thee willingly and freely to be thine forever. In the simplicity of my heart, I offer myself to thee this day.'[7]

A more contemporary statement might be this paraphrase of the words of surrender of a nineteenth-century Christian, Hannah Whitehall Smith: Dear Lord, I abandon myself to You. I have tried in every way I could think of to manage myself, to make myself what I thought I ought to be but have always failed. Now I give it up to You. I give You permission to take entire possession of me.[8]

In some cases the response is described as a powerful, dramatic but nonverbal experience. Fredrich Buechner says, 'Faith is not so much believing this thing or that about God as it is hearing a voice that says, "Come unto me." We hear the voice and we start to go without really knowing what to believe either about the voice or ourselves. And yet we go. Faith is standing in the darkness and a hand is there and we take it.'[9]

In that moment of surrender, although we may not realize it, we stand in an open doorway to freedom from our seemingly irreparable past.

We may see that we have always been as close to the reality, the loving acceptance, and the wisdom of God as if there were only some sort of membrane that needed to be popped, as at birth. We can now be released from the inner world of slavery to a relentless and misguided constructed life from which our reality-oriented souls have been excluded.

Imagine the spiritual warrior as a person, emotionally exhausted, isolated from herself and others through having tried to recreate the world to satisfy her own needs. From the darkness of her mind, this pilgrim reaches out toward what appears to be God. Sometimes in that moment people have spoken of a wave of light breaking into their darkness. It is as though a voice were saying through that light, 'You are accepted, accepted by that which is greater than you.'[10]

The language difficulties in trying to describe a profound experience of spiritual change are enormous. I think Goethe may have been close to the mark when he said that the greatest truths can only be expressed dramatically. God seems to have felt the same way in that the Scriptures are a drama primarily and not just a cognitive book of truth. But whatever the words or nonverbal movement signifying surrender, this deep spiritual change takes place when God's hand reaches from His drama into ours and touches us in an exquisite and inexplicable way that unlocks the inner prison of our souls. Perhaps only those who have been through the head-on collision of the constructed personality with reality, and with God, to the point of surrender can easily recognize the landmarks and language of response.

However it happens, when we do surrender, we get a glorious surprise, a sense of receiving the very thing from God that we always wanted. This seems like an impossible miracle because each person appears to receive a different thing, uniquely theirs, tailor-made to the needs of their own starving soul.

Some people receive a great release from guilt, a sense of forgiveness and new relatedness to God and people. Other people report that they gain a personal revelation to the meaning of life. They've been on a meaning search. Some, like me, feel that we have received security, love, or self-esteem. We had built an entire fantasy world of the dreams of success that were sure to get us this self-esteem – but did not. Still others gain personal courage to be who they need to be in a difficult relationship or job, or perhaps a deep intuitive realization that at last they have the freedom to become the self they vaguely dreamed possible, living in a less bounded and more loving and creative way.

In almost every instance, whatever is received seems to relate specifically to satisfying the particular frantic spiritual needs that person tried so desperately to meet through their constructed personality's performance. We receive, it seems, the answer to the particular questions that kicked off our inner journey!

Ironically, although we cannot *prove* this, when the soul is released and comes in contact with God, if often seems to play a joyous kind of soul music on the veins and arteries of our hearts like a harpist. The words to the soul song are some variation of: 'I know this experience is true because it fits the deeper reality of my intuition and experience!' When the sense of being accepted by God is measured by the reality-checking soul, the soul's response is often a resounding 'Yes! This encounter with God fits reality at the deepest level I've ever envisioned it!' That deep inner personal validation makes people willing to risk their lives to share their faith. No one (not even the shaming voices) can tell them that what they have found at the deepest level of their experience isn't true, because it's what they've always longed for and known in their souls at some subterranean level was in fact true!

Once Released, the Soul Knows What to Do

In the aftermath of surrender, the fear and the awful need to be in control and to be right are transformed into awe and relief. For the moment, the fear is gone. In place of the driven, exhausted person acting fearfully and compulsively through

171

the constructed personality, there emerges an inquisitive, good-natured, childlike part of us that apparently is listening for instructions from God. The freed soul is like an amazing and happy bird, a dove, or a homing pigeon. Our soul appears to know where to go once it gets free. It circles the heart a couple of times and then flies to the Godward door of our lives, welcoming God as our new source for truth, motivation, and practical direction.

Often the soul is filled with joy, realizing it has stepped through the doorway of its prison into its true place, connected to God – the dream of its life. It's funny how this works. Throughout their lives people may have nocturnal dreams of being somewhere and experiencing something they know they have never experienced before, yet at the same time they have an intimation that somehow they *have* been there or have had that experience. I remember such dreams about sitting in a class, or being on a vacation somewhere I'd never been, seeing a particular scene or sunset I'd never seen – but yet it seemed that I *had* been there. In a similar way, the minute the constructed personality crashes and totally surrenders to God, some people have a strong transrational assurance that God will be there for them and will continue to guide their steps and unlock their gifts – as if they had known all along these things would happen. For many people this is a very concrete experience of the gift of faith.

This surrender is not about have been 'bad' and becoming 'good.' It's about being accepted and loved as one is and having the door opened to a new perception of what is real and true. The individual has a whole new sense of relatedness with God and life in which he or she is not responsible for huge accomplishments or perfect performance in order to be enough.

My experience has been that this surrender can lead to the

discovering and unlocking of gifts and aptitudes – and the motivational energy to go for them – that God also planted in our souls from the beginning.

This is not to say that when one surrenders as totally as possible that the constructed personality is suddenly gone, removed. That would be a kind of perfection no saint has claimed.[11] Rather, this deep surrender leads to a 'power shift,' so that the executive officer is no longer the controlling, unreal, and defensive constructed personality but the reality-oriented, loving, God-centered soul that wants to bring all of one's life together to become an authentic, learning, truth-telling child of God.

But as we shall learn, the constructed personality can bide its time and reassert its dominance in an instant – if we do not learn new spiritual habits that constantly refocus our attention on God and being real.

16

Surviving the Crash: A Case History

A PARADOX ABOUT THIS JOURNEY AND THE PROCESS OF
freeing the soul is that it's not just for religious people seeking
fulfillment. Many men and women 'back into' this trip toward
reality and intimate relating to God because of drugs, alcohol,
broken homes, or vocational failure. It doesn't matter how
people reach an awareness of their powerlessness to fix their
lives. When their constructed personalities crash, they often
wind up on the secret adventure of the soul in its search for
God. It's as if *all* people are drawn to God by the inner
magnetic forces described earlier as the yearnings or longings
for fulfillment put into us at birth.

After the surrender, without the resistances and denial of the
constructed personality and its powerful, self-centered goals,
the notion of God often becomes much more clear, plausible,
and concrete to nonreligious people. When *anyone* finally
becomes conscious that God is for him or her – the personal
liberator from the painful consequences of a life focused on
something other than God – or when anyone experiences God

as the satisfier of those first magnetic longings, God may become that person's most important intimate personal reality.

When this happens, it can be like turning a page and finding oneself in a whole new chapter of life. For some this is a peaceful transition. For others with the newly released soul in charge, the feeling may be that of being catapulted scared spitless into a very stark world of reality, sanity, and hope.

That's what happened to me![1]

Nine years after that morning in 1976 when I had looked up at the statue of Jesus against the sunrise and realized that I had destroyed my marriage, that everything in my life seemed to be in a shambles, I was still trying to find out how a Christian who had failed could do something in order to thank God for His love and concern that had kept me going.

I had practically disappeared from public view and tried to put my personal and vocational lives back together. Having written a couple of books after the end of my marriage, it was difficult to face the fact that in the Christian marketplace I was not welcome. Many people did not want me to come and speak anymore either. Although I had confessed, asked God for forgiveness, and made what amends I could in my personal life, a lot of Christians rejected me. I could understand their rejection. After all, I'd sinned, broken the rules, and gotten divorced. But after having almost never before failed significantly in my life, it was very painful and lonely.

During the nine years after my divorce, I spoke and wrote to singles groups about the lostness and fears I experienced as a single Christian and how even a bruised relationship with God had saved my sanity. In 1977, a year after the divorce, I met Andrea Wells, and we were married in 1979. I was very grateful for a second chance with a wonderful person. And I went back to work.

I began to write again, and to lecture, and before long got busier and busier. But inside, things were still not right. I tried to put my humpty-dumpty constructed life back together. Because I wasn't aware that I had a constructed personality, I didn't know that I was in denial about my life's secret agenda to get self-esteem and love from people out in the world. All I knew was that after what had felt to me like a glorious and successful twenty years as a committed Christian, I was no longer accepted as a hero in the Christian world and was no longer invited to the large prestigious meetings. The withdrawal of esteem and the accelerating fear of failure interspersed with periodic experiences of rejection caused me to clutch and unconsciously begin trying to promote myself and my projects in a much less subtle way. But consciously I kept trying to do it right.

I prayed compulsively, read the Bible and everything else I could read that might speak to my condition, and tried to help people in trouble. Before long, however, I was once more driven in a constantly overcommitted schedule. Finally I was tired, bone tired.

How could I keep up this pace of speaking, writing, and counseling, given the enervating inner conflict I was experiencing? The gospel I believed in so sincerely had quit working for me in terms of providing the security, love, and self-esteem I had unconsciously set out to achieve. I began to get some threatening heart symptoms.

Finally in 1983 Andrea and I holed up in a house we had on Mustang Island. I walked the beach in the moonlight – and at last the tears came. I walked and prayed and wept over what seemed like the failure of everything. I knew I'd been converted in 1956 and that God had helped me find a new life. I'd sinned, confessed, and failed vocationally. Still I kept working hard to love people and do God's will. How, then, had that life failed to bring – if not success – at least the peace Christians were promised?

It was insane. I'd already had far more success than I had prayed for or dreamed of, but my shaming voices told me I had succeeded more than I deserved, more than I was supposed to. In failing morally, I had shamed my whole family and lost the esteem I'd sacrificed so much for. Now I was burned out and had returned to that familiar place of being over my head with commitments and feeling insecure.

For the first time I wanted out – out of the religious rat race. I had tried hard to 'come back,' to demonstrate that even with my confessed failure, I was at heart a good man. But the church would not have it. Finally I'd had enough rejection.

But now I had a new problem – how do you bail out on God? It didn't seem right to just leave the ministry, God's work, even though I was rejected, exhausted, and burned out from too much studying, witnessing, writing, and counseling. Leaving a business was one thing, but this was different. What finer thing could I go to than what I was doing in ministering to hurting people? Anyway it didn't fit my image to be burned out, because I had committed my life to Jesus. So I just prayed.

Then I tried going to prayer meetings and to counselors, and for a while I'd be a quieter burned-out person. But I never could shake the fact that there was an escalating war going on inside me – and I wasn't winning.

In 1985, I jogged the beaches of Mustang Island, poring over these painful memories and praying for understanding and guidance. I knew other Christians who were frustrated and had some of the same problems and drive for success as I did, and they didn't talk much about them either. Sometimes late at night some of us talked about our lives. I remember one very successful Christian writer and speaker who has great integrity saying privately late one night after a conference, 'You know the strangest thing has happened. I'm giving all these lectures on family life and my kids don't like me.' Someone else said they'd discovered that their kids were afraid of them. How could things like this be?

Then in the spring of 1985 something catastrophic happened. My 'happy, grateful, humble, witty,' constructed Christian personality began to fall apart and turn sour. Although I'd prayed to find places to witness and work with hurting people, I began resenting those who did call and make demands on me by inviting me to speak, counsel, and serve in our little mission church on committees. I was confused by my conflict about not wanting to speak. The awareness that I was fighting against the very things that made me 'successful' let me know that however good things might start to look again on the outside, my personal game plan to get self-esteem was not working at all. Finally my smile that covered the anger and fear in my stomach seemed plastic, even to me. I began to drink more than I ever had, to cover the pain and fear concerning my sense of impending doom.

As this confusion and inner conflict grew, my soul's voice got louder and louder, trying to blow the whistle on my unreality and the dissonance between who I'd thought I was and how I was living in my vocation. But I didn't understand what my soul's crying meant until I went for help.

Finally, in June 1985, I checked into a treatment center. I went for a work addiction, which seemed like a respectable, safe thing. But I found out all kinds of interesting truths while I was there – about myself; about my incredibly entrenched constructed personality, with its denial of everything that didn't support its image and goals; and my addictive use of work and alcohol as defenses against the pain and fear of failure and not getting self-esteem.

Part of the treatment process involved listening to people close to me who were asked to confront me with ways I had been behaving that hurt them, others, and myself – about which I was in denial. I had agreed not to interrupt the process or defend myself. Why should I fear learning anything about myself? I was the guy who thought he was almost totally honest. But I was told that I was dishonest, that I had selfish motives, and had hurt people by trying to control their lives, the people I loved most.

At first I couldn't believe I was these negative and harmful things my constructed personality abhorred. Yet I had been given specific examples of each dishonest, controlling, and compulsive behavior. Everything in me rebelled at seeing the unreality of my fine Christian personality. I was enraged, and inside I blamed the people who were confronting me for exaggerating.

After ten days of this I could not get to sleep at night. I felt enormous anxiety and fear. It was as if something horrible was happening to my body that I couldn't locate, as if I had a huge, pulsating cancer that was systematically devouring my vital organs. One night I finally dropped off into a fitful sleep, but I woke up with a start at 3:45 in the morning. The room was in total darkness except for the dim green display on my digital alarm clock. Still not totally awake, I looked up in a half dream and seemed to see a great steaming black blanket, dripping scalding water, and hovering just under the ceiling – black like evil itself. It was hot and suffocating, about to drop on me and snuff out my life. Although I felt like it must be my imagination, I didn't know for sure. I was terrified!

I stumbled out of bed and grabbed my Bible on the bedside

table as I banged and bumped my way into the bathroom in the dark so I wouldn't wake my roommate. I turned on the light and felt cold sweat all over my upper body. I couldn't remember ever having felt such terror before. I sensed that my life was at stake, the life I'd always known. At the time I didn't realize that my constructed personality was just standing there shaking like a condemned building, waiting for the huge round demolition ball to strike – one last time – and send my life crashing down in a heap! It felt as if the great steel ball was going to hit me and I'd be shattered into hundreds of pieces. I tried to look at the Bible, but I was too filled with fear and dread even to see anything. There were only lines of words.

Finally I hurried to the nurse's station. I wept, and the older nurse just held me like she would hold a child as I sobbed and sobbed. It was as if there were a giant tightly wound steel spring of pain at the center of me that was uncoiling and uncoiling. Then, some time later, still shuddering occasionally with fear, I finally got out the story of my frightening experience and powerlessness, and of what I had just realized about my denial, about my life.

Two hours later I was calm, though exhausted. I talked about what had happened. During those past several days my unreal constructed 'realities' had been confronted. God had used some courageous, loving people with some really tough love to finally break through my rock-hard denial. I saw the constructed personality I had built, and its lack of congruence. I saw, amazed and yet knowing it was true, that I *had* tried to control and change everyone's behavior around me to get them to meet my needs for esteem and love as a good father, husband, or friend. I had acted as if meeting these needs was their job – and God's job through my success. It was horrible to see how self-centered and controlling I had always been. This was the biggest ego insult of all, to realize that I was not the positive, sincere, and unselfish loving father, husband, and Christian witness I thought I was, and had sincerely presented myself as being. At long last my unreal constructed personality had crashed in pieces all around me.

The indigo shadows of the bluff on the other side of the desert were just starting to inch across the plain below when I turned to God in the pre-dawn light that morning in July 1985. With a childlike sense of humility and gratitude for survival – but with no idea of what the future might hold, I offered the stark new life I'd been thrown into (which I did not understand) to God: I had no reservations or dreams of success, no plans. I wasn't trying to get God to fix my relationships, or my vocation. I just surrendered my broken life, my family, and my whole future to God – no strings. I asked Him to show me how to do His will that day, one hour at a time.

17

Dawn, in an Upside-Down World!

Therefore, if any one is in Christ, he is a new creation,
the old has passed away, behold, the new has come.
2 Cor. 5:17

WHAT WAS I GOING TO DO? SITTING THERE AS THE DAWN broke that July morning in 1985, I thought, 'If the devious and controlling personality in which I have invested my entire life isn't Keith Miller,' and I knew for sure that it wasn't, 'then who am I going to be?' Even though I had seldom been conscious of being deceptive, I was ashamed of not having spotted my devious constructed personality and its desperate need for success and esteem. I'd never before been even close to the level of pain and shame I felt over behavior that led me to face this devastating reality and grasp what my life had been all about. I'd buried my brother and my parents – everybody I grew up with in my family of origin – by the time I was 28, but the uncertainty about the future caused by those changes was nothing like what I now faced.

But as I accepted these new realities about myself, about my denial and the unreal personality I'd constructed, I also felt a deep sense of peace. 'At last,' a small voice inside seemed to say, 'you don't have to pretend anymore, and God can pick up the pieces of your shattered past and help you live a new life based on the truth of who God made you to be.'

I'm convinced that this quiet, confident, small voice was the voice of God speaking through my soul as it had finally come out of its crushed prison cell beside my now crumbled constructed personality. That was, for me, the reality of my situation when I started out that morning at the treatment center.

The Voices Were Not Gone

The shaming voices were still telling me their old familiar message, 'This "new life" you think you have is a complete cop-out and proves you are a wimp! You fouled up again! You were doing fine! You didn't have to change. They set you up! You let them get to you! You just needed some rest and you'd have gone back and really succeeded!' Though I wanted to believe that changing wasn't necessary, I now knew the shaming voices were lying. My friends and family loved me and had told me the truth. As a matter of fact, they had risked a lot to tell me, and I knew they were on target. In the crash of my constructed life, my soul had urged me toward reality and now verified what my family had said.

Recently, I was reading Annie Dillard's Pulitzer Prize-winning book, *The Pilgrim at Tinker Creek*. In that book she cites the work of Marios VonSenden.[1] It seems that years ago, when Western surgeons discovered how to perform safe cataract operations, they traveled through Europe and

America, operating on people of all ages, giving them sight. Many of the patients seemed to have no notion of space, form, distance, height, or depth. When these patients did see, it confused a lot of them because they couldn't make sense out of the jumbled array of colors and shapes they saw. For these newly sighted, vision – like that of a newborn baby – was pure sensation without meaning.

But because these patients were adults, they could report what they experienced. What some of the formerly blind people did was to close their eyes and lick the object before them, or feel it, smell it, or listen to it or to get a fix on the object and tie it to their own previously blind experience. Before they closed their eyes and checked, many of the objects – even some very familiar ones – confused them, though they now saw the object clearly.

I discovered that in my own escape from 'blindness,' I too needed to check out, to reevaluate almost all my relationships and motivations as a result of the spiritual change I'd experienced. When I began to look at life through spiritual eyes, I had to find new words to describe the shockingly new, even the familiar, feelings I was having. For instance, as a father and husband, I had always thought sincerely that I was just 'helping people' close to me. I discovered that I really was continually trying to change them, to fix them, or control them, to get those good but hard-headed people to see or do things my way, which was often arbitrary and self-centered. During the first few weeks of my new life, I saw a number of realities like that through my soul's eyes as it moved toward becoming the new executive of my personality.

For a few days after this cataclysm and surrender, my life was like a trip to another planet. Men and women looked the same, but the snow was gone from the screen of my receiver.

People didn't scare me so much, because I wasn't defending or afraid of being revealed as inadequate. I saw that living out of a constructed personality had required a lot of surveillance and rationalization to make sure people didn't 'misunderstand.' In actuality, the surveillance had been to make sure they didn't *understand* the nature and depth of my unreality and manipulation. Now that I no longer had surveillance and self-justification as my primary stances, people came out of the woodwork as persons. They looked simpler, less threatening (and less threatened) as I related to them as a listener and sharer rather than as a writer and lecturer.

I was content just to walk around the next few days and watch people and listen to what they were saying. I also got to watch myself and listen to what I was saying, because I was like a child in a new world; I didn't know how to behave. Somebody would say something, and I would experience myself automatically thinking of a famous quotation that I could slip into the conversation to let them know I was smart, and also (my constructed voices said) to 'clarify' the subject under discussion for them. Instead, I didn't say anything. I watched myself keeping silent and listening to the other people, to what they were really saying, who they were. I had to smile as I realized that the conversations and the other people got along fine without my great wisdom.

I had a different set of questions about life and people now, because my constructed personality didn't seem to need to be the authority, the expert, in order to feel like somebody. I also didn't appear to have some place to rush to. I remembered how a good friend had said years before that I always looked like I was hurrying toward the men's room.

I felt very vulnerable and uncertain that first day, that whole week. When I would get insecure, I noticed that I jumped back into my constructed personality and tried to impress people. When I did, I discovered I was not comfortable with my former behavior and attitudes.

I loved the calmness, but I also felt strangely shy. I always feel very emotional and close to tears when I try to describe this shyness. Yet when I was aware of being shy, I felt good because something told me that 'that's who you really are.' There was much more congruence between what I was doing and what I felt myself to be during those days.

I finally understood why I had scored as an introvert on a psychological evaluation profile I had taken years earlier. I'm very introverted in my interior life, but in my constructed personality I had been operating as an extreme extrovert. Evidently I had behaved as an extrovert to gain love and/or approval, but inside in my soul I was the exact opposite. I apparently did the extroverted behavior in order to please other people or to get the esteem and success I wanted so desperately.[2] No wonder I had gotten exhausted as an outgoing traveling lecturer. Inside I was almost a total introvert.

When I'd finally seen the powerlessness of my constructed personality to make things right in my life and give me self-esteem, the awareness of the powerlessness to change had brought me to get help and then to surrender to God in a new and much more realistic way. In the aftermath I saw the insanity of my old agenda of being good and succeeding in order to get other people to give me the good feeling about myself that I now know only God can give.

But coming out of a lifetime of denial, of unconscious dishonesty with myself, how in the world could I begin to see my devious behavior among the ruins of the past? How could I find the courage to have the vulnerable, rigorous honesty I was told would lead me to intimacy, self-esteem, and self-love – the things my soul said God could deliver?

By the end of the first month after my surrender, I knew that much of what I'd learned in the past about living for God was somehow upside down. Did I dare to look at that apparent upside-downness in the Christian community where I found myself and see what it might mean to try to live through my soul? Ten years ago going counter to what appeared to be the constructed personality of the church sounded very lonely to me. I soon realized, however, that it's not my job to change anyone else – or convince them to live the discoveries revealed in the rest of these pages.

If you are happy with the way you are living and with your relationships and can't identify with any of this, I think that's great. If it's not broken, don't fix it. If you feel like you need to change your life, I see that changing as God's job and yours – not mine. But I will tell you a little bit about what I discovered as it relates to reorienting one's way of living after the kind of crash and surrender to God I have reported.

Part 4

Life with the Soul in Charge

Introduction to Part 4

AS I STARTED INTO WHAT WAS TO BECOME A SERIOUS REORI-
entation of my inner life, I wanted to see what was still real
and what hope there was for a future. I wanted to get rid of
my compulsion to control and fix people, the addictive behaviors I'd taken on to cover my personal pain, and the grandiose
habits I'd seen that were often done to show what a good
Christian I was. Although I wasn't aware of this, my deepest
longing was now to find out how to live with integrity, intimacy, and self-esteem.

It is evidently not necessary for everyone to go as far down
as I did before they are willing to admit that they are powerless and can begin the spiritual life of the soul. Some
constructed personalities may not have lost reputation,
money, and family, but may have somehow seen clearly the
painful direction their disintegrating constructed personality
was taking them. Sometimes such people can identify with the
story of someone whose constructed personality has crashed.
By hearing the stories of those who have lost everything, they

may be able to see the downward direction and trajectory of their lives and be grasped by the fact that they really are powerless to recover by themselves – without actually having to lose all their possessions and relationships first.

When they get those insights about their lives and experience their powerlessness, some people may be able to surrender to God and get converted or changed in a way that frees the soul and starts the new chapter of their spiritual story.

18

Intensive Care Unit for Souls

I FINALLY REALIZED THAT I'D UNKNOWINGLY LOST INTEGRITY, intimacy, and self-esteem one small piece after another as I continued to deceive myself and blindly stepped on people as I tried to control them. After the crash and surrender, I discovered that in order to recover the soul's kind of integrity, intimacy, and self-esteem, I had to reverse the processes by which my constructed personality had destroyed or damaged those things in my life (see chapters 9 and 10).

For me the struggle against turning my future over to God and the final giving up was a little like going through major surgery without an anesthetic. When the agony was over, I had said a yes that echoed down into the depths of my heart, like a pebble falling into a well. I was exhausted. What I desperately needed was a safe place to get reoriented: to recover the integrity I'd lost without knowing it, to experience some acceptance and healthy intimacy, and to find the energy to get on my feet in every area of life.

But where does a man who's been in denial go to discover

how to be honest with himself and others – maybe for the first time in years? Most educational and religious groups I knew about simply didn't seem to know how to deal with such raw spiritual issues openly, and many didn't even think it was appropriate to talk about them.

Reestablishing Integrity

I saw that my soul's imprisonment had seriously impaired my connection with reality, my integrity – because of the denial, control, and projection of my constructed personality. I wasn't sure I could tell when I was deceiving myself or other people. But I was sure that I didn't want to do it any more. For me, finding healing involved two essential elements. *First*, I had to find a place where I could see integrity in action, where it was safe to risk being open. I needed a context in which I could tell my own truth as I discovered it, and where I could test my new trust in God. *Second*, I had to learn to see the specific nature and extent of my *unreality* so that my authenticity could be reestablished.

Finding a Safe Place to Grow

In short, I needed a safe place in which to begin living in reality. As shameful as it was to admit, the truth was that I could not share my reality with integrity – especially the defects, character defects, and the accusations of the shaming voices – until I could see what they were, because I'd hidden many of them from myself. In the constructed worlds in which I had operated, it was not safe (vocationally, personally, or emotionally) to share vulnerably the negative and unacceptable parts of

194

what was really going on with me. It had seemed suicidal. Even after my surrender the possible reactions of others around me to my truth and the power of the shaming voices felt very threatening. So after realizing I could not do this changing by myself, I risked joining a truth-telling spiritual reorientation group.

The first time I sat in this group I was frightened and uncertain.[1] I was almost as afraid of being known and judged by that group of strangers as I was of going back to the painful prison of my previous unreal life. I was very uncertain as to how I might fit in. I'd been a Christian for many years and a Christian public speaker and writer for almost thirty. But I was such a fearful loner in my heart that I felt out of place and anxious with these seemingly relaxed and unafraid people. They appeared to accept each other, and me, without the usual reticence I'd always had before. My heart was beating as if I were going to be the keynote speaker at their meeting, instead of just a visitor.

The rules the leader read were certainly different. I heard that if I shared (and it was my choice whether to share or not), I was to talk only about myself, not anyone else. Also, we were asked not to give advice to anyone who shared, nor to interrupt him or her for any reason, and to keep everything said in the meeting confidential. This was not what I was used to, and I was suddenly very alert. But then when people began to share their stories – the good, the bad, and the ugly – I was shocked and *really* scared!

A man got up and told us something he had done to his business partner that was dishonest and embarrassing to his family when it came out. When he finished talking he seemed to be very relieved, and sat down. There was a part of me that could hardly keep from jumping into the silence and saying, 'You shouldn't tell that! Someone will gossip and use it against you!'

But just then people in the group said, 'Thanks for sharing, Harry.'

'Thanks for sharing?' I thought, 'Were they insane?' then: 'My gosh,' I thought in amazement, 'they aren't judging him! They're acting as if he's done them a favor sharing that bad stuff.' I shook my head. This was an upside-down world. How could confessing something like that help me?

But as I sat in the back of the room and thought about what the man had just said, I remembered something I'd done in a business situation years before that I had not even thought of since it had happened. I had not been caught and (I said to myself) my transgression was 'a relatively small thing compared to his.' But as I thought about that statement I realized that I had carried my 'insignificant' dishonesty around in my unconscious mind for forty years! 'Hmmm,' I thought. 'It must have been a little more important to my soul than I'd supposed.' As I reflected on this later, I realized that in my constructed personality I had put the whole incident in denial – at a time in my young business life when I had thought I was totally honest. I had denied my dishonesty so thoroughly as a Christian businessman 'leader' that I hadn't thought of it for about four decades – and this man had told about his dishonesty the week it happened, before some men (like me) whom he didn't even know! What was going on here? I was amazed to realize that just the experience of hearing this stranger share his reality, his failure had popped something out of my unconscious mind that my soul indicated to me I'd needed to confess and give to God years ago.

I came to see that such a truth-telling group, where everyone has agreed not to repeat anything said outside the meeting, could accomplish some miracles in the process of helping people like me who really want to reorient their lives and come out of denial to reestablish integrity. I got very excited.

Here was a way, at intense spiritual but no financial cost, that we surrendered people could learn to see the denied painful material from our past – so that we could offer it to God.

Learning to be Spiritually Honest

Now that I had found a safe place to begin, I wanted to learn more about how I could see my own unreality and deal with the negative and abusive traits about my life and character that I had already discovered in the 'crash' process.

Because my constructed personality had been adamantly against sharing in a vulnerable way, I saw that I was going to have to learn how to turn that message around and become spiritually honest with others in this group. I was told to be patient, that it might take a long time to learn to be emotionally and spiritually honest. This seemed like a strange thing to say to a Christian who'd written a number of books about trying to live with integrity. But it was true; because as I listened, I saw how much of my life was no doubt still in denial. Also I realized that sharing that vulnerably is very threatening at first. Soon, however, it became absolutely apparent to me that such personal honesty was going to be essential for the recovery of integrity and the growth of my soul – and the rest of me.

As the weeks went by, I saw a number of surprising facts. When I listened to other frightened but growing surrendered people and shared my own secrets in a supportive, truth-telling group, at least three things happened that proved to be very important to recovering some of my own reality and integrity.

SEEING BEHIND OUR DENIAL

When another person shares a specific example of a character defect or self-centered behavior from his or her own life, that person becomes a mirror in which I may see myself, may actually see behind the wall of my denial and locate not only past but current denied actions and character traits, things I might never see by introspection, or if preached to. I had been taught, like many religious people, that we, like the Pharisees, can't see the log in our own eye. But what they didn't teach me – even in seminary – was that preaching at people's denied sinful behaviors may only drive them further out of sight into denial. Instead of convincing the listeners to change, such preaching may only cause the listeners to recall other people's similar sins and prompt them to pray for those others to change.

In truth-telling groups, however, I saw how God used the witness of one person sharing a sin or harmful behavior from his own life to reveal to the other people in the group their own similar (but denied) harmful behaviors and sins. Since I saw that there was no finger-pointing or shaming attitude in the person sharing, I was willing to open the shutters, doors, and windows of my own well-protected, denied life to let more truth out where I could see it! You can check this principle out right now by asking yourself if the frank illustrations in this book have revealed to you any behaviors in your life like the ones I have shared. If so, you may have taken a step into the healing process I am describing.

SHRINKING THE SHAMING VOICES AND FINDING HUMILITY

To my surprise, as I listened and began to share as vulnerably as I was comfortably sharing, I realized something incredible about the shaming voices. The only power they have, the only weapon in the shaming voices' arsenal with which to cripple our self-esteem and integrity, is the threat of revealing the shameful acts, character defects, and attitudes of our past. Psychologists have long known that our secrets control us. But when we voluntarily share these secrets in a spiritual community, the content we share and the power of the voices to shame us lose their strength. Eventually, to me, the shaming voices seemed to get weaker.

This happened, as I, trembling with the lifelong fear of being seen as inadequate, brought struggling into the light things that were shameful to my constructed personality. The shaming voices seemed to shrink almost visibly when I admitted to others in that safe group things that had always seemed so shameful to me. One day I told the group that I am almost completely self-centered and how that plays out for me. Later, when I was alone and my shaming voices said, 'You are a totally self-centered jerk!' I smiled and replied to the voices, 'Yeah, that's what I just told the group!' The first time I did that it seemed to take the wind out of their sails and the 'faces' of the shaming voices wore a very confused 'look' as they quieted and withdrew. That was when I knew I was in new growth territory with my soul!

In a practical sense this sharing in a safe, nonjudgmental atmosphere made me *less* afraid of people – not *more* afraid of them as my constructed personality had predicted. I was less afraid of being discovered as inadequate and less fearful about honestly facing and admitting mistakes as they happened – all of which I now know are very important parts of recovering integrity and self-esteem.

This process of owning and dealing with one's shameful past and present can lead to one of the great virtues of the soul: humility.

My constructed personality thought that humility was a kind of false groveling. If I were being humble that way, I might have said on this page, 'I can't imagine I am the one getting to write about the soul to you! Some of you are *far* more talented than I,' etc., etc., etc. With my soul released, now I might say instead, 'Some of you have more ability and know more about the soul than I. But if you feel that way, you can write your own book. I've been thinking about this material for years, and I'm writing this one.' That sounds rude to my constructed personality, but from the soul's point of view humility is facing and being willing to share things as they really are in your own life – when you choose to – the happy, positive things as well as the pain and sin. I now believe that all things that are true are a part of God's reality, and are not to be automatically suppressed or denied. (Although all things are not equally appropriate to share with everyone.)

For example, Rob was a young Christian father who wanted very much to pass on to his children an authentic faith. He was just beginning to sense the dissonance between his own behavior and his inner life. When he prayed with his little boy, Jamie, Rob taught him the rote prayers he had learned as a boy in Sunday school, ending with 'God bless Jamie and Mother and grandmother. Amen!' Each night Jamie repeated the exact same prayers after him.

One evening Rob and his wife were at odds with each other and had a loud argument at the dinner table in front of Jamie. Rob stalked away after delivering a cutting sarcastic remark to his wife.

When it came time to pray on their knees beside Jamie's bed, Rob realized that reality was he needed to confess to God before Jamie, because Jamie had heard the abusive language he'd used toward Jamie's mother. So, although Rob felt great resistance to sharing that he'd been wrong before his son, in his prayer Rob did confess, 'Lord, please forgive me for being mean and sarcastic to Mother. Help me not to do that again. Amen.' In the dark Rob sensed Jamie's discomfort as he rapidly blurted out the usual prayer.

To Rob's chagrin, the next night he did virtually the same thing at dinner and stalked away from the table again. But when the small honest voice within him suggested that he confess a second time beside Jamie's bed, Rob's constructed personality rebelled, saying, 'No, don't do that, Rob! If you confess to doing the same bad thing twice in a row, Jamie won't ever respect you as a Christian father!' But by that time they were kneeling beside Jamie's bed in the dark.

After a few seconds hesitation, Rob began, 'Lord, I am so sorry I shouted at Mommie and put her down again tonight. I don't want to be that kind of man. Please help me to not do that!!'

There was a poignant silence in the dark. Rob was thinking his telling the truth had lost his son somehow. Then Jamie said hesitantly, 'Dear Lord, please forgive me for pushing Don in the mud at school in front of everyone and telling the teacher I didn't do it!' Jamie made a real confession of a lie he had been hiding for several months.

When Rob had prayed through his constructed personality and not through his soul, he only taught Jamie to do the same. But when Rob failed, and then confessed a real sin that Jamie knew was true, Jamie learned a lifetime lesson for his soul: that it was safe to confess threatening things to God, and to his father.

Evidently only a humble person living in reality is teachable in the spiritual realm of the soul, because spiritual is all about reality – ours, God's, and other people's. And if I am not living in the light of my own personal reality – the awareness of the controlling, self-centered, or abusive parts of me – I cannot change and make decisions with integrity that will lead me to intimacy with people close to me and with God (see 1 John 1:5–7).

ADDING A NEW SET OF INNER VOICES

Besides shrinking the shaming voices when I reveal my unacceptable secrets in a truth-telling group, I also hear people say to me things like, 'Thanks for sharing! Thanks for being honest! We're glad you're here!' Those accepting and affirming people – after a while – were actually introjected into my head as a new set of voices, advocates to counteract the shaming voices! These new voices are those of nonjudgmental surrendered people who've heard my worst and yet who love me, affirm me, and reward me for being honest instead of only for being perfect, the way so many of us felt we were judged as children. Because I, and most of the people I've talked to, despaired of being perfect and hid behind our constructed personalities, we seldom if ever were affirmed for being ourselves.

Reparenting

I've learned to take these new positive voices with me wherever I go. They become reinforcements on my side – for the first time – in the inner battle with the shaming voices. To know I could have voices inside arguing for me in the battles for self-esteem was wonderful news! I had seen early on as a child that I could never be perfect, but in truth-telling groups I saw that I *can* learn to become more honest. These loving, accepting voices were *reparenting* me, accepting me just as I am, by accepting my soul's halting attempts to be authentic. When those people, who had no manipulative stake in controlling me, really cared for me – imperfect as I admitted to being – I could begin to love myself! Their gentle caring brought me real spiritual strength and resolve to have integrity, something I never could have counted on. So when these new reparenting voices came inside my life, they began to change the balance of power in the inner warfare with the shaming voices that had tyrannized me as far back as I could remember.

A Cloud of Witnesses

Historically, Christians have seen these positive inner voices as a heroic 'cloud of witnesses' who love God and accompany us through history, affirming and loving us (see Heb. 12:1). The church has sometimes called such supportive people (living and dead) the communion of saints. And the late Carlysle Marney spoke of these positive introjected voices as our 'balcony people' who counteract the shaming voices from the basement of our lives.

These new positive voices in my life were representing the larger spiritual community. They knew my imperfection and failures and loved me anyway. This experience of love coming from people who know my imperfections is fulfilling a lifelong yearning for acceptance that seemed impossible to my isolated constructed self. These positive inner voices are living witnesses who by their very presence to my inner life counteract the lifelong expressed opinion of the shaming voices that I am unlovable and don't deserve love, or even to have friends. These new on-our-side voices, and the people they represent, offer us – for being our honest selves – the very esteem we tried too hard to earn by successful performance through our constructed personalities. We begin to get a glimpse of the new spiritual family Christ came to bring us.

The most profound miracle concerning these positive loving voices is that with them in our lives we don't have to *earn* esteem anymore, and we never have to be alone again.

19

A Spiritual Laboratory for Intimacy

IT IS EASY TO SEE WHAT AN ENORMOUS HELP THIS SORT OF sharing can be in the recovery of intimacy. In the first place, the sharing of one's reality in one place where the listeners just listen and share, but don't condemn, shame, or try to fix the one sharing, is one definition of intimacy. As I learned to be more honest about my reality, the truth-telling orientation group became a spiritual laboratory for learning and practicing intimacy.

The startling paradox to me was that I'd always been afraid that if you knew me you would not like me, and certainly not love me. But I discovered that when people first stood up to speak in these truth-telling spiritual orientation groups, I was often indifferent to them. However, by the time they finished sharing the painful stories of their out-of-control constructed personalities and how they were now trying to learn to live for God, I liked them, then loved them. It was incredible! Because of that experience of loving them, I could believe that they could love me once they really knew me. This awareness that people could love me almost never happened when I was living in my play-it-close-to-the-vest constructed personality – even though people had said they felt close to me and cared for me for years as I had tried to share from the platform. But I just hadn't been able to believe them until I'd heard others share in these truth-telling groups and found that I could love them.

What often happens is that after a long time of attending and sharing at such meetings, the integrity and intimacy become so natural that they almost accidentally spill over into our close relationships outside the meetings.

For example, Wil had been raised in a family in which the men did not express affection. He'd wanted to as a boy, but he'd never seen either his father or grandfather hug a family member or express love verbally, so he didn't either. For many months in a truth-telling group, Wil kept hearing other men talk about how they had been learning to express affection at home. One evening he came home, hung his hat and coat in the closet, walked into the kitchen, and said to his wife in front of their four children, 'Annette, I've realized recently how much I love you, and I don't know if I've told you.' After about two seconds Annette turned slowly around from the sink: tears were streaming down her face.

It may take a long time from such a beginning for Wil and Annette to be able to share with the openness Wil has learned to share each week at the spiritual reorientation group. Still, he made a beginning and broke a three-generation taboo.

The fact that the constructed person sometimes chooses an inappropriate mate does not have to be a tragic waste. When the surrender to God takes place and the soul is in charge, the past can be accepted as both parties commit themselves to finding and doing God's will. Couples can face the reality of their differences and begin to build on the foundation of their shared powerlessness to make everything right and their common new adventure of growing up in God's family of maturing souls. Truth-telling groups can provide much support, security, and friendship while intimacy is being built or rebuilt in personal relationships outside the group.

If couples begin the surrendered life together, the process may work faster. But for the recovery of intimacy between couples and family members, the truth-telling group can be a wonderful school. For authentic intimacy to take place in long-term relationships, someone has to learn how to risk sharing vulnerably first. The group provides a very valuable, safe place to see integrity and intimacy modeled and a place to practice being honest appropriately about one's feelings and harmful behaviors. By hearing honesty being tempered by love in the sharing of surrendered people, one learns a certain gentleness and humility. As strange as it may sound, if one begins trying to be honest in a personal relationship without such a group, it may be disturbing, frightening, or offensive to the other person.

This ability to be honest about one's own mistakes and transgressions is also very good training for confessing and making amends, a more advanced expression of the cleansing, healing power of integrity and intimacy with other people and with God.

When I heard in a truth-telling group how one man's insistence on his partner's accepting his expectations had ruined a relationship, I became more and more motivated to risk changing my super-adequate, always-right (about the past, present, and future) stance and to start sharing my pain and fear instead. As I did so, I began learning how to allow God to heal my primary relationships.

For example, as I mentioned earlier, my constructed self has always been a virtual self-justification machine. If someone criticized me, I felt that I had to make sure that they, too, were at least partially wrong, so I wouldn't be the only one feeling inadequate and shameful. One day a member of my family was describing the way I had hurt him in a situation that had taken place years ago. He described in detail my self-centeredness and devious behavior. I knew that the event and behavior he described was true – and that was very painful for me to face. But unfortunately for him, he got some of the details wrong – mistakes which, if true, would have meant I had been even worse than my actual abusive behavior had been.

So, as he was continuing to elaborate on how my behavior had hurt and angered him, I began thinking about how I could straighten him out about 'the facts' he had presented. All of a sudden, my soul began clamoring for my attention. I stopped my defensive, shaming, and self-justifying planning, and asked myself the question I have learned to ask of my soul in conflict situations: 'What's reality here?' And the answer was: 'The point here, Miller, is that this guy is right. You were a selfish, controlling, power-playing you-know-what. But now you are planning a way to discredit and turn the tables on this person who loves you but is trying sincerely to express his pain and anger. Instead of listening to a description of the impact your behavior has had on him, you are working on how to make him feel inept, ridiculous, and *wrong*. By dumping your shame on him this way, you think you can avoid feeling your own pain, shame, and guilt. Reality is that he is describing a time in which you *were* being a real self-centered so-and-so! *Don't quibble about the details!* Just face the painful truth about the impact of your behavior on this person without trying to minimize it or justify yourself.'

I hated to hear that, but I knew that was what I needed to do. So instead of attacking, I steeled myself and did what I had seen people in truth-telling meetings do. I admitted that I had been controlling, self-centered, and abusive, even though

I felt great pain, guilt, and shame about admitting it. I also confessed that I had seen that the behavior he was describing had been a lifelong pattern of defensiveness and self-justification. I then asked for forgiveness.

This kind of sharing is viewed by constructed personalities as stupid and inappropriate. After all, they have been trained – or learned through experience – that it is not safe or effective to share honesty at this depth. Never mind that our earlier 'honesty' may have been about *other people's* faults and not about ours at all. No wonder it hadn't been safe to share and we got painful results. Consequently many of us have spent a considerable amount of energy rationalizing and hiding our weaknesses and mistakes. I still do this a lot – especially if I get too tired and discouraged when my life doesn't seem to be going well. If you feel strongly resistant to the idea of learning to be honest in this way, you are perfectly normal. It is a frightening idea. But for me, it was only as my constructed personality crashed and I surrendered to God that I realized the preposterous lengths to which I had gone in order to hide my imperfections, to be 'right' in my relationships, and to try to get my way.

I've learned that several things can happen as a person like me listens to others in the group share stories about the rigidity of their constructed expectations and the way they tried to control their mates to get their way.

After the crash and surrender, people may quit having to succeed and be right about everything. Amazingly, sooner or later, the growing soul may just not sweat getting its way all the time. I used to think I knew how most things should be done much better than my wife did. To my surprise, as I realize I don't have to defend everything I do now, I've come to realize that she knows much more about a lot of things than I do. I've seen that some formerly loaded issues, like whether she wants her next car to be black or white – or bright purple – are just not important to me now. It's her car and her choice. But in my constructed personality, a purple car in *my* driveway was unthinkable. It would have reflected on me as a successful wearer of natural shouldered Brooks Brothers clothing.

Not having to be right all the time is one of the most delightful changes that crashing and surrendering can bring. For years I had long arguments with those close to me about all kinds of things. After ten minutes I often couldn't remember the issue, but I kept arguing because I knew I was right, and I kept right on trying to win. Then one day, after my wife and I had both been attending truth-telling groups for several years, Andrea and I were having a doozie of an argument. But this time I *really* knew I was right. It was about an issue I'd just checked out. Just as I was about to lower the boom on Andrea with my superior proof, she suddenly realized that I was right. She looked at me for a couple of beats and then said with a grin, 'Ha, ha, ha. I'm wrong and you're right!' I looked at her for a few seconds, sort of stunned. Then I said slowly, 'Wait a minute, wait a minute . . . maybe *I'm* wrong.' Then we both laughed. (Andrea later told me she heard another woman tell how she'd said that to her husband in a similar situation.) The startling thing to me was that as obnoxious as I'd always been about having to be right, Andrea was willing simply to swallow her pride about being wrong and use her friend's lighthearted words to say so.

Although we still get crosswise and argue, when one of us recognizes that we're wrong, that one smiles and says, 'Ha, ha, ha,' and the argument is usually over. This new ability to admit being wrong had seldom happened before we saw our constructed personalities and I saw my insistence on being the always-right center of our shared world.

I could give dozens of examples of how the process of

regularly attending spiritual reorientation groups and being committed to growing spiritually in one's relationships to God and others can change one's life.

Here is a (composite) example about a large, very shy man named Jack, who reported: 'At first I was too afraid to share with the group the fact that I was not honest about my overeating habits and about the fact that I try to shame my wife, Betty Lou, to keep her from acting so superior about her ability to diet. But I finally shared those things in a meeting, and, over the next few meetings, I told more and more of my story concerning the devious ways I have acted to assure the maintenance of the unreal life I'd built. After the first meeting, I was surprised to see that other people there told me they felt closer to me when I shared, and that they felt safe to tell me who they were and what they had done imperfectly in their life.

'As time went on, individuals told me, in private, shameful parts of their lives that were like mine, and a change took place between me and them. There was a softer, more accepting look in their eyes. Our sharing was almost like a conspiracy. Not long ago another man and I were recounting some bizarre things we had done in our past, and we laughed together until I almost cried at the ridiculous lengths we had gone with our surveillance and self-justification. I realized suddenly that this was the most imtimate I'd ever been with another man.'

Very gradually over the months and then years, Jack became so accustomed to sharing honestly in that men's group that slowly, one person at a time, he began to tell his family members honestly about his overeating and other failures. And now, after a long hard road, Jack and Betty Lou are sharing their fears, frustrations, and hopes with each other and working out their current differences face to face. They report that they are happier than they have ever been, even though it's still not easy for either of them to be vulnerable to the other about some of their more intimate fears and failures.

As a former graduate school junkie, I had learned a surprising truth about spiritual healing and growth from people like Jack and Betty Lou. For the soul, spiritual growth doesn't progress as fast through study and analysis as it does through simple personal risking and story telling.

The wonder to me is that as people share real stories of their unreal constructed personalities' tragedies, sins, and failures without trying to manipulate to get esteem, a kind of peace or serenity usually permeates the group like a spiritual perfume. As they share the tender positive discoveries they are making, the ones sharing are often accepted and even loved by those who hear them. Such hesitant sharers are not only practicing integrity and intimacy for their own soul's growth, but they may also become carriers of the kind of loving closeness they have always longed for with those they love.

Once the doorways to integrity and intimacy have been opened by the soul's nudging us toward an intimate life of reality, how do we keep the inner communication lines open and keep growing spiritually?

20

The Soul's Kind of
Communication with God

I'VE BELIEVED ALL MY LIFE THAT COMMUNICATION WITH GOD,
if real, is one of the most mysterious and uniquely personal of
all human experiences.

I Had it Right, Just Upside-Down

I've prayed since I was a small child. But soon after my
surrender to God I discovered that my prayer life had been
upside-down (along with much of the rest of the world I'd
known). When my constructed personality had been in charge
(and playing God), I had prayed as if God were made in *my*
image to help me accomplish *my* agenda (and He wasn't doing
His job too well).

I remember being told years ago to, 'look at God as if He
were a business partner when you're praying.' I'd even used

that analogy when teaching people how to pray. (At least I was smart enough to call Him a 'senior' partner.) But my praying betrayed me. I prayed as if God were a junior partner who had inherited a lot of money. I had the ideas and made the decisions, but He had the bucks to put them into practice.

Most of my constructed personality's prayers for myself and those for other people had been to inform God of my instructions concerning the outcomes He should produce during the week ahead. I was trying to get God to do my will. Now I realize the purpose of prayer is to get *me* to know and do *God's* will. But here is the catchy part: sometimes I told God about those for whom I prayed, and then asked Him to alleviate the pain in their lives – including mine. Sounded good – and very Christian – to me.

But after the crash, as I began to learn how to pray from my soul's perspective, I realized that when I prayed for other people to change in a certain direction, I was assuming that I knew what they needed in order for God's will to be done. In my unwitting arrogance I was really praying that *my* will for that person would happen. When I prayed that someone would get a certain job or marry a specific person or not marry a specific person, I was praying that God would do my will. But in truth-telling groups I began to see how skewed my will really was.

Let me give you an example of how this works. A close friend named Cynthia told me that she had prayed that her son, Peter, would not marry a girl she didn't think was good enough for him. Peter, however, was very angry at his mother and married Angela anyway. Some years later Cynthia told me how wrong she had been about Angela. Her son, Peter, had been killed in Vietnam, and shortly after that Cynthia's fifty-five-year-old husband, Derek, died as a result of a heart attack.

Cynthia said to me, 'I guess I thought I was smarter than God when I prayed that Peter wouldn't marry Angela. Now she is really an angel to me. Not only is she a wonderful mother to their three children, but she has continued to visit me over the years and bring the children. She has even invited me to go on vacations with them all.' Cynthia paused and looked out of the window thoughtfully before continuing, 'I'm certainly glad God didn't answer my arrogant and snobbish prayers about Peter's marriage to Angela.'

Recognizing that my prayers for the success of my ministry and for things other people should be or do were often an extension of my constructed personality's attempts to control people and circumstances was a real shock! After what I've learned about reality through my soul, I now believe that prayers for one's self and others are fine for spiritually healthy people. But such praying is very dangerous for a controller like me with a lot of energy – who has been masterminding a controlling Christian constructed personality for years.

I now see that about the best thing that ever happened to me was when my constructed personality's prayers and those prayed by my family and friends about alleviating my pain and bringing me new success were not answered in the way they were prayed. Consequently my constructed personality's efforts failed, and I crashed and burned – and finally surrendered. In my crash, that failure that I saw at the time as the tragedy of my life, my soul was freed and I got a chance to go on an exciting adventure with some of you.

Probably many people I prayed for actually needed to walk into their pain until they realized they were not God. Yet I hate it when people close to me are hurting (or anyone, for that matter)! I learned to tell God so, as part of my attempts at spiritual and emotional honesty. But my question became: How could I pray for others yet avoid my tendency to control them (and God) by advising Him of my 'solutions' for these hurting people?

Put All in God's Hands

As I began to feel more centered in my soul, I learned a new and wonderfully simple way to pray for others that for me has been a very freeing thing. I cup my hands together as if I were going to drink from a river. Then in my imagination I put the people I want to pray for in my cupped hands, one at a time. I imagine God sitting before me with His hands cupped together like mine, and I take each of the people I love – my wife and each grown child, my grandkids and other family members, friends, and others I pray for (including myself) – and put them in God's hands, one at a time. I release them into His care – with love – and I don't say anything.

I've realized at long last that I don't *know* what's best for other people and the adventure of their souls. They may need to face the pain they're in or even to crash and burn. And I may need to walk with them and help them if that happens. I'm not talking about deserting people, just the opposite. This way of praying allows me to get out of God's way and to set these people free (from my controlling tentacles) to live out and learn from the drama that God has given them to experience in their souls. In short, I'm resigning from trying to be the producer and director of their show.

A few years ago, when one of my daughters' husbands died as a young man, my daughter and I were sitting at her breakfast table after the funeral. She began to talk about all she had to do now that the funeral was over, about her husband's will, about their children, and about the future. Inside I was hurting like crazy for this, my little girl, now grown, whom I love so

215

much. At almost any other time in her life, my super-father self would have interrupted, jumped in several times, and told her, 'This is what you should do about that,' or 'I will take care of this or that task,' as she mentioned them. But this time my soul whispered, 'Be still and listen.' After some time, when she finally wound down, she exhaled and looked at me with what appeared to be a lot of love through her tears. Then she said, 'Dad, I feel like that's the first time you ever really heard me.' We hugged and we both wept.

For the soul, much of prayer is listening to God and His other children.

21

Listening: Can You Really Hear God?

AFTER I STARTED PUTTING PEOPLE IN GOD'S HANDS, I TURNED my prayers toward trying to find God's will for my life. In a truth-telling meeting I heard a man say that in order to learn God's will he had begun to listen for God with the purpose of getting concrete direction from Him about how to live. That would have sounded very spooky – and even naive – to my constructed personality, except that Paul Tournier had told me that is what he did. He listened to God for ten minutes a day and wrote down everything he heard. Now my soul was urging me to try the listening prayer, so I decided to try it for a month.

The first morning I couldn't get my mind to be quiet. All kinds of images of mundane things I had to do came to mind. The shaming voices said, 'We knew it! You're a religious nut!' I was really getting tense.

So I closed my eyes and prayed that God would please help me quiet my nervous motor-mouthed mind so that I could hear His voice among all those to which I had been listening all my compulsive life. I saw at once how very different listening was

217

going to be from my previous approach to prayer – which had been more like calling God on my one-way Rolodex-guided prayer phone and telling Him what He should do for me and all the other people I wanted Him to fix.

Then I started to listen. The first thing that came to my mind was, 'Get your car washed.' I was a little irritated. I had expected something spiritual. As I kept listening, I got a whole 'to-do' list of things like that. I went back to one of my mentors, who said, 'Well, you've evidently been on the wrong station for a long time, listening to everything else. So just keep listening quietly a while and write down *everything* you hear. It may take some time to tune your mind into the right station for you to begin to hear God.' So I decided to keep listening that way for ninety days.

How God Slipped into my Datebook Planner

One day early on, I realized in my listening time that I had a big-time resentment and then I saw some reruns of a lustful fantasy. I called my mentor and said, 'These things can't be from God!'

My friend said, 'Don't be too sure. Transfer them to a prayer list, telling God you'd like help with resentment and lust. This listening is a good way to get to the real issues you need to pray about.' So I listened and wrote – everything. And although I am not in any danger of being nominated for sainthood, over the years these particular areas of my life have, for all practical purposes, been resolved much of the time.

After some months I found that I could plan my whole day during the first five to seven minutes of my ten-minute listening time. Now, almost ten years later, virtually everything I need to do in my day comes to me and I write it down in a very few

minutes. Unless something new comes in to the office by telephone, fax, e-mail, or snail-mail, my day is planned. After the
ten minutes, I put the list in order and do it. At first, besides
producing all kinds of distracting images and messages, this
listening time brought forth a list of things to do that was twice
too big. When that happened, I was told to 'carry over the
undone items to the next day, until they get done.' This process
helped me see how grandiose I am about how much I think I
can do in a day – and eventually caused me to cut my commitments drastically. I never would have thought the soul's
reality-oriented prayer would bring God into my datebook
planner where my real life goes on. But that's the way it is
working for me.

'Voice Mail' Love Notes

But most days I had three to five minutes of my ten-minute
listening time left. So I kept listening, and one day I heard this
in my mind: 'Keith, you're a precious child and I love you.' I
wept. Wow! I'd never heard anything like that in my own
quietness. I didn't know if that was God's voice or my soul's,
but now that I believe my soul is that part of me nearest to
God, it really doesn't matter.

What I'd heard before were things like, 'You're not enough!'
'Hurry up on your book!' and 'You dummy, your to-do list is
still too long!' I began to hear various different messages about
my being loved: 'I love you and always have!' 'I'm glad you're
coming to Me now without all that other baggage of your too-
busy life.' And although it was difficult for me to write down
such positive things, I wrote them down anyway. I couldn't
explain it, but God was using these messages to give me the
courage and strength I really needed to try to live for Him.

At first I protested to myself and to God: 'This has got to be unreal because it can't be true!' And I wept again as I wondered if it was all right for me to love myself. Then I remembered that Jesus had said to 'love your neighbor as yourself' (Matt. 19:19). I laughed as I realized I'd done just that – loved my neighbors as I loved *myself*. I'd been a mighty poor neighbor-lover, since I didn't love myself very much at all. Now I began to have hope that maybe I could love people – because when I heard a voice inside saying repeatedly that I am loved, and I remembered the affirming voices of the truth-telling groups, I began to believe that God loves me.

I still heard the shaming voices too. They said, sarcastically, 'You're making these loving messages up because you've got a big ego!' But somebody I respected had said to write it all down and not to pay any attention to the familiar negative voices. So I wrote it all down. Wherever the new positive messages came from, I began to believe them, and my soul seems to affirm them as being reality for me.

But on many days there were still three to five minutes to listen.

Messages from the Dream Box

All my life I've kept a corner of my mind set aside, like a cedar chest used for storing cherished clothing or treasures, for thoughts about things I'd like to do – someday. Yet I had always thought that most of them would come to nothing except to provide entertainment for my imagination if I ever had time to bring them out and dust them off. Amazingly, I began to hear messages in the last few minutes of my listening time that related directly to these dreams.

For example, several years ago, for months as I listened I heard, 'Write songs.' I'd chuckle as I'd write that down because my singing voice is such that when my children were growing up they never wanted me to sing when anyone was around – even at the football games. But since the message didn't go away (extraneous things tend to disappear over time), I began to think that I should check into writing songs. I didn't know anyone who wrote the sort of pop songs I had in mind, but shortly thereafter I met a songwriter at a wedding party being given for Heather Huffman and her husband-to-be, Tommy Pierce. Heather and her family were longtime friends. When I asked Tommy what sort of work he did, he said he was a songwriter.

My face must have ignited when I blurted out, 'I've been wanting to write some songs!'

I could see the concerned look on his face, as if he were thinking, *who is this old guy who's going to bug me about writing songs with him?*

So I backed off, embarrassed, saying it was good to meet him.

But several weeks later he called, and after finding out we had a surprisingly good rapport, we wound up writing a musical play, *Home Is Where You Are.*[1] We have even premiered it at several conferences across the country. Although it may never be a financial success, cowriting those songs opened the doorway to the publishing of a print and audio book of Texas ballads I've written.[2]

Later in my listening time of prayer I heard, 'Write a novel,' and I am close to finishing that now. Another book that came out of my experience with this kind of listening, *Ten Minute Magic*,[3] is about this process of listening to God to discover your own dreams that may be locked in your unconscious mind, and then making a plan to accomplish them.

And finally (some time before the series of lectures I did on which this book is based), I heard while listening, 'Write a book about the soul.' At that time I had no material or idea about how to do that.

Some people hear more traditionally spiritual or religious things when they listen for God – like 'Check out seminary' or 'Start an adult class at church about the soul' (as I did).

As I've told others about this process of writing down what comes as you listen, they have reported very interesting things. One man I'll call Jeremy wrote to me three months after he'd written down, 'Become an artist.' He said he'd gotten an art teacher to tutor him. Now, ninety days later, he had painted and sold twenty-three oil paintings. Another person, a father, wrote to say that in listening he'd realized that he ought to turn loose of his grown son's life, and he finally put the young man in his cupped hands symbolically and laid him in God's hands. He told me they are now being reconciled after years of 'clashing constructed personalities in the night.'

Reality for me is that this prayerful listening meditation means that God and my soul are interested in what's real for me to be and do in the real world.

Messages About Loving Others

Besides things to do in my daily life and my vocation, I have gotten nudges to call or write someone. Sometimes I discovered that person was sick or in trouble, but more often I just had a good visit with him or her. My soul is teaching me that, for me, love is experienced through reaching out to people in prayer and walking with them in the pain and the ordinariness of life.

These are just a few of the many different ways of looking at prayer and living that have come to me so far from the now wise but somehow childlike executive in its new administration in the secret life of my soul.

22

The Unfolding of the Plot

IN THESE CHAPTERS I HAVE DEALT WITH A FEW OF THE surprising things I have discovered and shared with others as I experienced trying to live with my soul in charge. Some additional things I've had to find out that you may encounter are:

- I had to learn a specific process of confession and forgiveness to handle the irreparable past and deal with the ever present tendency to build a new constructed personality and supplant God in an unguarded instant.
- I had to find work with a spiritual mentor to help me see and deal with denial and new spiritual challenges.
- I had to discover ways to begin to learn to love others and myself, and to relate to soul mates, family members, and people not even on a spiritual journey, blending love with the process of dealing with reality, so that I can be a better neighbor-lover and friend.
- I had to find a way to develop a positive attitude toward affirming my own and other people's creative hopes,

dreams, and aptitudes God had put in our lives in potential. I found, too, that this quieter part of me can be a
pensive and persuasive presence for goodwill and caring
and for affirming others in utilizing their gifts and aptitudes, which my fast-moving constructed personality
didn't have time for.

- I had to find the meanings of church and worship that
  had eroded over the years, the medicinal use of words
  and symbols as means of dealing with the Phoenix-like
  constructed personality and the soul's growth.

- I had to learn again how to read the Scriptures and other
  books, and memorize passages that bring strength and
  resolve to the soul.

- And last, through my soul's eyes of faith, I had to find a
  way to deal with the fact of my own inevitable death, and
  decide what I believe about a life beyond that ending.

These and a hundred other things I have discovered and
tried to accept and to deal with realistically during this past
decade. But I have a clear sense that this book is finished now.

If you are interested in a spiritual adventure with God, you
may want to think or pray about your life, about the possibility of your having a constructed personality, and about the
freedom or incarceration of your own soul. You may want to
reflect on integrity and intimacy in your life and relationships,
and about your inner sense of acceptance and self-esteem – or
the lack of these things. You may want to set out to find or
start a small truth-telling community where your healing from
the past can begin.

But be very cautious about starting such a group without
definite ground rules for protecting the anonymity of all
members, and to stop the tendency within the group meeting
itself to talk to people about what they shared, to alleviate

their pain with 'answers,' and/or to fix their problems.

The bottom line of the reorientation process I have been describing came for me one morning several years into the adventure. I woke up and my voices started in on me, as they so often do, before I was even fully awake: 'You're behind on your work! The book you are writing stinks! And you're not only old, but your hair's coming out and you're ugly!'

But then something took place on my inner stage that had never happened before. My soul was standing, holding onto the cross (which represents God to me) in the center of the stage. I noticed that the soul was much larger than I'd remembered (no doubt from assimilating all that vitamin-like reality we had been facing). Then my soul, with all of the introjected voices of my fellow adventurers, turned on the now shrunken but still hostile shaming voices, and shouted in unison: **SILENCE! YOU ARE NO LONGER MY HIGHER POWER! GOD IS MY HIGHER POWER!**

In that moment, self-esteem was born in my life!

I know that in a way, I have just begun the spiritual adventure in my soul. I know that I'll always have inner battles and that there will continue to be new revelations, crises, and surrenders in the ongoing life of my soul. But now I have new tools, weapons to face and change the self-defeating adversaries of fear, inadequacy, denial, and self-doubt. Some of these weapons are: a loving spiritual community of other people on the soul's adventure – where truth-telling is normative; a relationship with my family in which some of us are becoming soul mates on the journey; and a relationship with God that gives me a strong desire to face reality and live my whole life for God.

Epilogue

ON AN EARLY JUNE MORNING IN 1996 IN THE SOUTH TEXAS hill country, I was standing on a bluff, looking out over the rugged rocky landscape. The heat was already rising off the sand around the silent limestone formations between the scrub live oak trees in the distance.

Our entire family, fifteen of us – three daughters and sons-in-law, seven grandkids, and Andrea and I – had just spent four wonderful days together at a dude ranch. We were leaving that morning.

I thought about the twenty years since I'd sat in front of the huge bronze statue of Jesus – not many miles north of where I now stood – and started the wild spiritual adventure of searching for my soul by facing my pain and denial and being introduced to my lonely, self-defeating constructed personality. I felt a gentle wave of gratitude flowing through my life with the soft wisp of a breeze that brushed my face.

Behind me, I heard the gravel crunching under cowboy boots as one of my tall grown daughters, the youngest, walked up and stood beside me. She looked out over the top of the scrub oaks, above the heat waves, at the small town of Bandera in the distance.

'Hi, Dad,' she said, smiling.

I turned, and my heart melted a little, as always. 'Hi. Pretty morning,' I replied, as I looked back at the broad vista that stretched to the horizon in front of us.

She nodded and then said, 'What's happened to you, Dad?'

I started to tighten up, then realized that I didn't have anything I was defending, and relaxed. 'What do you mean, honey?'

'Well, you've looked like you were – at peace, this whole time we've been here.' She said the words carefully so I'd know she was serious.

I thought about how tense I'd always been with my family, making sure I could defend the tall constructed white knight personality. Then I turned and looked at her directly and smiled. 'That's because I have been at peace,' I said quietly.

'Well,' she said, starting back to her cabin to finish getting her kids packed, 'I just want you to know that it has not gone unnoticed!'

'Thanks,' I said, and I could almost hear my soul laughing, because I hadn't noticed I was peaceful, but I had been. I was just being happy and listening in awe to my amazing and delightful family.

As I turned to go tell Andrea that the car was packed, I stopped and looked at the light blue morning sky. There were towers of billowing white clouds moving slowly westward. I said under my breath, 'Thank you, God!' And I heard a small, young-sounding voice inside me, saying, 'My gosh, maybe we're going to grow up after all!'

Notes

Introduction

1. Claudia Wallis, 'Medicine for the Soul,' *Time*, July 1994.

2. Karl Meninger, *Theory of Psychoanalytic Technique* (New York: Harper and Row, 1964), 14.

Chapter 1

1. See William Temple, *Studies in St. John's Gospel* (London: Macmillan, 1963), 24.

Chapter 2

1. *Merriam-Webster's Collegiate Dictionary*, 10th ed., s.v. 'soul.'

2. Carl Jung, *Psychological Types* (London: Routledge & Kegan Paul Ltd, 1953), 593.

3. Robert Johnson, *We* (San Francisco: Harper San Francisco, 1983), 160.

4. Thomas H. Naylor, William H. Willimon, and Magdalena R. Naylor, *The Search for Meaning* (Nashville: Abingdon Press, 1994), 93.

5. Paul Tournier, *The Meaning of Persons* (New York: Harper & Row, 1957).

6. Thomas Moore, *Care of the Soul* (New York: HarperCollins, 1992), xi, xiii.

7. From a personal letter to the author dated December 12, 1996.

Chapter 3

1. This fantasy description of prenatal, birth, and early postnatal 'experience' is concocted from existing knowledge, theories, and impressions of practitioners in this field. For an excellent and more scientific view of this area of life experience, see Margaret S. Mahler, Fred Pine, and Arnie Bergman, *The Psychological Birth of the Human Infant* (New York: Basic Books, Inc., 1975).

2. Otto Rank, *The Trauma of Birth* (Belmont, Calif.: Wadsworth Publishing Co., 1994).

3. Richard D. Grant, Jr, and Andrea Wells Miller, *Recovering Connections* (San Francisco: HarperCollins, 1993). (Carl Jung called this guidance system the 'Self.')

Chapter 4

1. Ibid.

2. Ibid.

3. Ibid.

4. Antonia Wenkart, Jean Rosenbaum, and Natalie Shainess, *National Enquirer*, 13 December 1970.

Chapter 5

1. For a more complete discussion and examples of how each of the four yearnings can be misdirected, distorted, or denied, see Grant and Miller, *Recovering Connections*.

Chapter 6

1. See chapter 1, section on 'Sin and Evil,' page 20.

2. Tournier, *The Meaning of Persons*, 123f.

3. I realize that the terms 'guilt' and 'shame' have been used by some to mean the same thing or to mean things different from those just described. In this book, however, I am using the term 'guilt' to mean the feeling a person has when he or she does something against his or her moral code or values, recognizes the action as a transgression of a moral code, and feels guilty. But that person can still feel like a *good person* – who has done a wrong thing. Shame, as distinct from guilt, can occur when a person makes a *mistake* that is not necessarily against any moral code at all – like giving the wrong answer to a question on an exam, or failing to turn off the freeway at the correct exit. Although the sensation of shame feels like guilt, the person making the mistake has a sense of being a *bad* person (instead of a good person who has done something wrong as in the case of guilt). Shaming voices are more painful and destructive to the child because they attack his or her self-esteem *directly* by calling the child 'no good person.' The soul does not shame the child, it only *calls attention* to immoral acts or unreal behaviors that evidence a lack of integrity.

Chapter 7

1. The ability to keep a secret is an enormously important *positive* step in the developing process of a child's individuality, boundaries, and growth. For example, it is appropriate for a developing child to keep certain things secret from

parents in order to become a healthy adult. Although we could spend a lot of time clarifying that process, what I am focusing on here is the kind of secret-keeping that leads to the creation and maintenance of a false and (from a spiritual perspective) counterproductive personality, and the repression and denial of the child's reality that can follow.

In normal development a child first learns to keep a secret; then later, as a second movement toward maturity, he or she gains enough self-esteem and security to be able to choose to *share* secrets with safe people in intimate relationships. In fact, choosing to share secrets at a good time with appropriate people is a strong benchmark of emotional maturity. However, when the threat of the rejecting shaming voices or caregivers is great enough – especially if there is not adequate modeling, outer support, or a sense of safety for the sharing of secrets – then some of the negative effects of being able to keep secrets may develop.

There are other situations that create in a child the need to keep secrets. These can come from forms of child abuse. Perhaps a parent threatens to withdraw love from or physically harm a child if he or she doesn't keep a secret about the parent's inappropriate behavior (e.g., an affair, secret drinking, or some sort of physical or sexual abuse of the child) from the other parent, family members, and outsiders. Or perhaps a molester threatens to harm or kill the child if the child reports the molestation. In this book, however, I am describing something else – the child's inner and uncoerced decision to build a false personality to avoid the inner shaming voices and to feel more adequate socially.

2. Carl Jung, Paul Tournier, and others have postulated a positive 'persona' or 'person' that each of us constructs unconsciously to get along with others in the world. They do not see the persona as a lie necessarily, but as an intermediary

between inner experience and outer demands. Because of the complexity of trying to describe this hybrid, I will refer to the experiencing child separated from the soul as representing the persona. The child is not meaning to be evil when he or she constructs a false personality, but when that constructed personality is clearly built of characteristics the child-soul doesn't feel are intrinsic to its reality, the constructed personality becomes a lie, fabricated in response to the attack of shaming voices on the esteem of the child.

3. I am aware that much of what I attribute to the constructed personality is what is generally thought to be what Freud described as the 'ego.' To the extent that all defenses are thought to be functions of the ego, this will be true here also. But when the battle of the soul with the constructed personality is won by the *soul*, it is *possible*, I believe, for a person to eventually have the soul as the executive of the personality, with only a small element of the ego's defenses remaining as healthy boundaries.

4. As I noted before, the child could (and in some cases does) choose to confess and might discover the esteem rewards for that. Or the child could refrain from confessing but decide not to lie again. This is part of the socialization process. It is healthy to be able to choose to have privacy and keep certain things secret, and to make certain harmless adaptations to family or society's norms (that one doesn't feel natural about). For example, my father was so against most of the policies of President Franklin Roosevelt that we could set him off into a tirade several hours long by agreeing out loud with some of the positive things Roosevelt had done. As a family we agreed finally not to talk about Roosevelt since we had so little time with my father and didn't want to spend it listening to charged emotional tirades. We felt this was a harmless avoidance because my father's feelings were irrational and apparently

unchangeable, and we weren't even interested in trying to change his thinking about the subject.

Such secrets and adaptations can be positive and even necessary to maintain one's membership in a family or society. But the problem arises when these secrets and adaptations are self-defeating because they cause the person to lie and continually misrepresent his or her authentic values, thoughts and feelings, thus making continuing intimacy, spirituality, and emotional growth extremely difficult, if not impossible. In the drama I am presenting about the secret life of the soul, many children make the very different choice of constructing a false but credible personality in denial – because of the threats of rejection.

5. Paul Tournier, *The Strong and the Weak* (Philadelphia: The Westminster Press, 1963).

6. At one time I was almost exhausted with the unreality of my constructed extroverted personality. I was traveling constantly, speaking before crowds of people, being the 'master of ceremonies' leader of conference centers, and leading several small groups. I took a highly respected psychological personality measuring battery that included an introvert/extrovert scale. On that scale a score of 'one' indicates that the person tested is virtually a total introvert, and a score of 100 would reveal a total extrovert. To everyone's amazement, I scored 'one.' At the time my constructed personality was almost a total extrovert. I remember answering every question with a deep longing to be alone and escape the crowded driven life I was living. I do not know whether what would normally be measured in terms of personality types more nearly reflects the constructed personality or the soul, but I am convinced that my pain and the repressed longing of my soul was accurately reflected by that scale.

Chapter 8

1. We have learned in many ways that what was considered medically normative in certain diagnoses is really not healthy. When my cholesterol was first measured years ago, it was 260. The examining physician said, 'That's not too excessive. We consider anything below 250 to be a safe risk.' Later, however, when people in other countries were measured, it was discovered that levels above 200 were risky. It seems that the elevated cholesterol in Americans was much greater than the heart-healthy people in the rest of the world that some U.S. physicians had not seen that what was normative in the U.S. was really dangerous. That's what I am saying about the constructed personality's seemingly 'normal' behavior. What is often thought to be innocent dishonesty and posing can be spiritually devastating to one's entire life and close relationships, or to the life of an educational, religious, or political institution.

2. For example, we in the United States sometimes insist that countries receiving our monetary assistance clean up their racial problems or lose our help, yet at times when such demands have been made, our own cities were in flames because of *our* racial conflicts. In our national constructed personality, we evidently do not notice such contradictions.

Chapter 9

1. For a more comprehensive study concerning how intimate relationships break down and what can make them well, see J. Keith Miller, *Compelled to Control: Why Relationships Break Down and What Makes Them Well* (Deerfield Beach: Health Communications, 1997).

Chapter 11

1. This compulsive use of work (including religious work) or some other behavior or chemical to cover the pain caused by not facing our reality is the source of virtually all addictions.

2. I am not talking here about a planned intervention in a family with outside help to confront a family member and give him or her the choice of getting help or leaving the family. This kind of intervention, which results in the out-of-control family member going to a treatment facility, often works very well. See Vernon E. Johnson, *I'll Quit Tomorrow* (San Francisco: Harper & Row, 1980), 48ff.

Chapter 12

1. Thomas Gordon, *Group Centered Leadership* (Boston: Houghton Mifflin Company, 1955), 85.

2. Since no one seems to get rid of a constructed personality *completely*, human beings in this life evidently never have a totally 'pure and intimate' spiritual relationship with God – or each other.

Chapter 14

1. Paul Tournier, *A Place for You* (New York: Harper & Row, 1966), 162.

2. John Knox, *Limits of Unbelief* (New York: Seabury Press, 1970), 84.

3. Francis Thompson, *The Works of Francis Thompson, Poems*, 2 vols. (New York: Charles Schribner's Sons, 1913).

4. Augustine, *The Confessions of St. Augustine* (New York: E. P. Dutton and Company, Inc., 1951), 1.

5. Bertrand Russell, *Autobiography 1914–1944* (Boston: Little Brown, 1967; London: Allen and Unwin, 1968), 96, also 36 and 21.

6. Grant and Miller, *Recovering Connections*.

7. For a dramatic biblical picture of this sort of crisis of the will and surrender, see the story of Abraham's being asked to sacrifice his adored son, Isaac (Gen. 22).

8. Ernie Larson, in a conference, Edina, Minn., Nov. 16, 1990.

Chapter 15

1. Carl Jung, *The Structure and Dynamics of the Psyche, Vol. 8 of The Collected Works* (New York: Pantheon Books, 1960).

2. J. Keith Miller, 'Analysis and Comparisons of Religious Conversions and Peak-Experiences' (Master's thesis, University of Texas at Austin, 1971).

3. Dietrich Bonhoeffer, *The Cost of Discipleship* (New York: The Macmillan Company, 1960), 53.

4. John Stott, *Basic Christianity* (Grand Rapids: Wm. B. Erdman's Publishing Co., 1962), 130.

5. Alfred North Whitehead, *Religion in the Making* (New York: The Macmillan Co., 1926), 16f.

6. Knox, *Limits of Unbelief*, 87.

7. Thomas à Kempis, *The Imitation of Christ* (London: Collins, 1957), 253.

8. Hannah W. Smith, *The Christian's Secret of a Happy Life* (Old Tappen, N.J.: Fleming H. Revell Company, 1968), 39.

9. Frederick Buechner, *The Magnificent Defeat* (New York: Seabury Press, 1966), 42.

10. Paul Tillich, *The Shaking of the Foundations* (London: SCM Press, 1949), 162.

11. As I pointed out earlier, I believe each soul is unique, so also are each soul's journey and crises. Therefore each person's resolutions that result from this sort of conversion experience

can be experienced in different ways. Evidently, there is no absolutely prototypical journey.

Chapter 16

1. Although I believe that many points in my own story illustrate some general principles in the life of the soul, each person's experience will be different in specific ways. It is not my intention to present my experience as a prototype, but only as an illustration of certain aspects of a much more comprehensive and many faceted process.

Chapter 17

1. As referred to by Annie Dillard in *Pilgrim at Tinker's Creek* (New York: Harper Perennial, 1988), 25.

2. After my constructed personality crashed, I found myself being a more open and gracious person because I felt more at ease with people than I ever had and didn't feel as compelled to be the extroverted center of attention anymore.

Chapter 18

1. In these groups the participants only share their stories of how they discovered their own twisted, manipulative, and self-centered constructed personalities. They tell about the ways in which they were in denial and how they hurt other people and themselves through their dishonest, controlling, or immoral behavior. When they have told the story of their past, they tell what led to the failure of their constructed life and how they surrendered or how they got to the group. Once they tell their conversion story, they share the ways in which they are making new discoveries of previously denied habits and behaviors and how they are trying to confess these things and make amends, how they struggle in their present relationships with God and other people on their soul's

journey. They share the strength, hope and practical things they are learning to help them to become more honest and loving – and stay close to God. The chairperson for the day may suggest a topic like 'fear' or 'intimacy' or 'communication with God' and people share their experience, their difficulties, and the hope and help they are finding about that topic.

Chapter 21

1. Keith Miller and Tommy Pierce, *Home is Where You Are* (Austin, TX: Villa Publishing, 1993).

2. Keith Miller, *Highway Home Through Texas* (Orleans, MA: Paraclete Press, 1993).

3. J. Keith Miller, *Ten Minute Magic* (New York: Cadell & Davies, 1989).

SEVEN SPIRITUAL LAWS OF SUCCESS by Deepak Chopra

'A must-read'
New York Times

Based on natural laws which govern all of creation, this book
shatters the myth that success is the result of hard work, exacting
plans, or driving ambition. In *The Seven Spiritual Laws of Success*,
Deepak Chopra distils the essence of his teachings into seven simple,
yet powerful principles that can easily be applied to create success in
all areas of your life. Filled with timeless wisdom and practical steps,
this is a book you will want to refer to again and again, for within
its pages are the secrets to making all your dreams come true.

'A Virtual Reality tool-kit for the 21st-century spiritual traveller'
Peter Guber, Chairman, Sony Pictures Entertainment

A Bantam Hardback
0593 04083 X

CREATING AFFLUENCE by Deepak Chopra

'Wealth consciousness is a state of mind, a sense, not of believing,
but really knowing that what we need is available to us . . . should
you read this book and take to heart the steps that are clearly laid
out, you will discover that life is easier and more abundant than
you ever thought possible'
Richard Carlson, bestselling author of *Don't Sweat the Small Stuff*

In this remarkable book lies the secret to creating affluence.
According to Deepak Chopra, affluence is our natural state, and
the entire physical universe with all its abundance is the offspring
of the unbounded, limitless field of all possibilities. In *Creating
Affluence* he gently fosters the wealth consciousness needed to tap
into this field and with clear and simple wisdom presents a step-by-
step plan for creating affluence and fulfilment in all areas of life.

'A delight and the source of much inspiration'
Body, Mind, Spirit

A Bantam Hardback
0593 04495 9

ANAM CARA by John O'Donohue

'Words of wisdom . . . a heady mixture of myth, poetry, philosophy . . . profound and moving' *Independent*

When St Patrick came to Ireland in the fifth century AD he discovered that where the Christians worshipped one God, the Celts had many and found divinity all around them – in the rivers and hills, the sea and sky, and in every kind of animal – an ancient Celtic reverence for the spirit in all things which survives to this day.

Irish poet and scholar John O'Donohue uses an intuitive approach to spirituality and shares the secrets of this ancient world. Here you will learn how to reconnect with the treasures that lie hidden in your own soul, how to discover your individual nature and understand the 'secret divinity' in your relationships.

'This book is a phenomenon . . . a book to read and reread forever' *Irish Times*

A Bantam Paperback
0553 50592 0

THE LEFT HAND OF GOD by Adolf Holl

'What a brilliant idea, brilliantly realized! . . . A fascinating and important book'
James Reston, Jr, author of *The Last Apocalypse*

In this divine biography, Adolf Holl examines the influence of the Holy Spirit in the context of Christianity, Judaism, Islam and the secular world. Interweaving scholarship with religion, myth and culture, Holl expertly traces the powerful effect of the Spirit on men and women over the course of centuries. The result is quite unlike anything written before.

'I was instantly hooked. The concept is ingenious, the writing lucid and the story unfolds like a saga'
Professor Harvey Cox, Harvard University, author of *Fire From Heaven*

A Bantam Paperback
0553 81192 4

A SELECTION OF NON-FICTION TITLES
PUBLISHED BANTAM BOOKS

THE PRICES SHOWN BELOW WERE CORRECT AT THE TIME OF GOING TO PRESS. HOWEVER TRANSWORLD PUBLISHERS RESERVE THE RIGHT TO SHOW NEW RETAIL PRICES ON COVERS WHICH MAY DIFFER FROM THOSE PREVIOUSLY ADVERTISED IN THE TEXT OR ELSEWHERE.

04495 9	CREATING AFFLUENCE	*Deepak Chopra*	£9.99
04083 X	THE SEVEN SPIRITUAL LAWS OF SUCCESS		
		Deepak Chopra	£9.99
40324 9	PERFECT HEALTH	*Deepak Chopra*	£12.99
17332 4	QUANTUM HEALING	*Deepak Chopra*	£10.99
18090 8	UNCONDITIONAL LIFE	*Deepak Chopra*	£9.99
50593 9	A CHILD OF THE DAWN	*Gautama Chopra*	£5.99
50662 5	SIMPLE ABUNDANCE	*Sarah Ban Breathnach*	£9.99
34539 7	HANDS OF LIGHT	*Barbara Ann Brennan*	£19.99
35456 6	LIGHT EMERGING	*Barbara Ann Brennan*	£19.99
81192 4	THE LEFT HAND OF GOD	*Adolf Holl*	£7.99
50537 8	AWAKENING THE BUDDHA WITHIN		
		Lama Surya Das	£8.99
50592 0	ANAM ĆARA	*John O'Donohue*	£7.99
04493 2	ETERNAL ECHOES	*John O'Donohue*	£15.00
50634 X	THE SOUL'S CODE	*James Hillman*	£7.99
50527 0	ANATOMY OF THE SPIRIT	*Caroline Myss*	£7.99
50712 5	WHY PEOPLE DON'T HEAL AND HOW THEY CAN		
		Caroline Myss	£7.99
40902 6	THE CELESTINE PROPHECY	*James Redfield*	£7.99
50370 7	THE CELESTINE PROPHECY: AN EXPERIENTIAL GUIDE		
		James Redfield & Carol Adrienne	£7.99
50418 5	THE TENTH INSIGHT	*James Redfield*	£7.99
50555 6	THE TENTH INSIGHT: AN EXPERIENTIAL GUIDE		
		James Redfield & Carol Adrienne	£7.99
50637 4	THE CELESTINE VISION	*James Redfield*	£7.99

All Transworld titles are available by post from:

Book Service By Post, PO Box 29, Douglas, Isle of Man, IM99 1BQ

Credit cards accepted. Please telephone 01624 675137
fax 01624 670923, Internet http://www.bookpost.co.uk
or e-mail: bookshop@enterprise.net for details

Free postage and packing in the UK. Overseas customers: allow £1 per book (paper-backs) and £3 per book (hardbacks)